This is where　　　　　　　　　　　　ne Jersey
went to worm ...　　　　　　　　　　　04.
Nancyjane developed & operated her own
wildbird rescue hospital from 1996-2001
supervising a volunteer staff of 25 people
and rehabilitating on average of 450-birds
of 80 species each year. The hospital was
closed when Grandpa Jersey was diagnosed
with lung cancer & required care. Rather
than reopen the hospital Grandma decided
to volunteer in centers around the world.
She also took on the political side & was
President of The Wildlife Rehabilitation
Network of British Columbia until she
moved to Australia to live in 2007. with
her partner Owen Preston in the Hunter
Valley N.SW.

Jirrahlinga

This book is about a remarkable woman, Tehree Gordon, and about Jirrahlinga, which began in the mid 1970s as five nondescript acres, a cottage and a couple of sheds at Barwon Heads on the southern coast of Victoria. Since then, without government funding, Tehree has built it into a model Wildlife Sanctuary complete with animal hospital, from which she runs an Animal Rescue Service.

The book is also about our wildlife, the birds, the mammals, the sea creatures and reptiles which are brought to Jirrahlinga. It tries to share something of the inestimable rewards that come to those who are lucky enough to know them and care for them.

Tehree's lifelong commitment to animals, and especially to wildlife, extends to humans as well. Handicapped, rejected and disadvantaged humans, children and adults, are taught to care for the wildlife at Jirrahlinga and in turn are helped by them.

The Sanctuary's name, *Jirrahlinga*, is an Aboriginal word meaning 'to find a home for a kangaroo' but in fact it finds a home for so much more.

BY THE SAME AUTHOR

The Girls
(1997; 2nd impression 1998)

The Shikari
(1998)

Alice and Sin
(1999)

Bloodstock
(2000)

(All published by Hudson Publishing)

JIRRAHLINGA

THE STORY OF AN AUSTRALIAN
WILDLIFE REFUGE, ITS CREATOR, ITS
CARERS AND ITS INMATES

ROBIN LEVETT

HUDSON
HAWTHORN

HUDSON PUBLISHING
The publishing division of
N. S. Hudson Publishing Services P/L
89 Stevenson Street, Kew, Victoria 3101

First published 2002
Copyright © Robin Levett 2002

Typeset by the publishers in 11/14 pt Palatino
Cover design by Arteffects, Kew

Printed by Southwood Press, Sydney

National Library of Australia cataloguing-in-publication data:

> Levett, Robin, 1925- .
>   Jirrahlinga : the story of an Australian wildlife refuge,
>   its creator, its carers and its inmates.
>
>   ISBN 0 949873 85 3.
>
>   1. Gordon, Tehree. 2. Jirrahlinga (Wildlife sanctuary).
>   3. Wildlife rehabilitators - Australia - Biography.
>   4. Wildlife veterinarians - Australia - Biography.
>   5. Wildlife refuges - Australia. 6. Wildlife conservation -
>   Australia. 7. Wildlife rescue - Australia. I. Title.
>
>   636.0832092

Contents

PART ONE	Tehree	1
1	Bushfire	3
2	Tehree's Jirrahlinga	17
3	Growing Up	25
PART TWO	The Wildlife at Jirrahlinga	39
4	Kangaroos and Wallabies	41
	Kangaroos	43
	Wallabies	52
	Raising baby kangaroos and wallabies	54
5	Wombats	58
	The Common Wombat	68
	Raising a baby wombat	71
6	Koalas	73
	The Koala	80
	Raising a baby koala	84
7	Possums	88
	The Common Brushtail Possum	94
	The Common Ringtail Possum	96
	The Sugar Glider	98
	Raising a baby possum or Sugar glider	100
8	Monotremes	101
	The Echidna	101
	The Platypus	106
9	Seals and Dolphins	111
	The Australian Fur-Seal	126
	Southern Elephant Seal	127
	Dolphins	128

10	Reptiles	130
	General notes on reptiles	136
	Snakes	138
	Lizards	141
11	The Birds	143
	The Sulphur-crested or White Cockatoo	145
	The Laughing Kookaburra	149
	The Australian Magpie	152
	The Emu	156
	Raptors	157
	The Silver Gull	161
	The Australian Pelican	162
	The Australasian Gannet	164
	The Fairy Penguin	165
	The Cape Barren Goose	169
12	Outsiders	170
	The Dingo	170
	The Fox	173
PART THREE	Jirrahlinga today	175
13	Rescue, Release and Euthanasia	177
	Jirrahlinga's Animal Rescue Service	177
	Rescue for the Layman	179
	Release	183
	Euthanasia	186
14	Reading Your Animal	189
15	Wildlife at Work	195
16	So You'd Like to Run a Sanctuary?	207
	Feeding convalescents	207
	Tehree's Routine (and yours, if you run a Sanctuary)	211
	The Rescue Service	212
	Hospital Equipment:	214
	R.I.P.	216

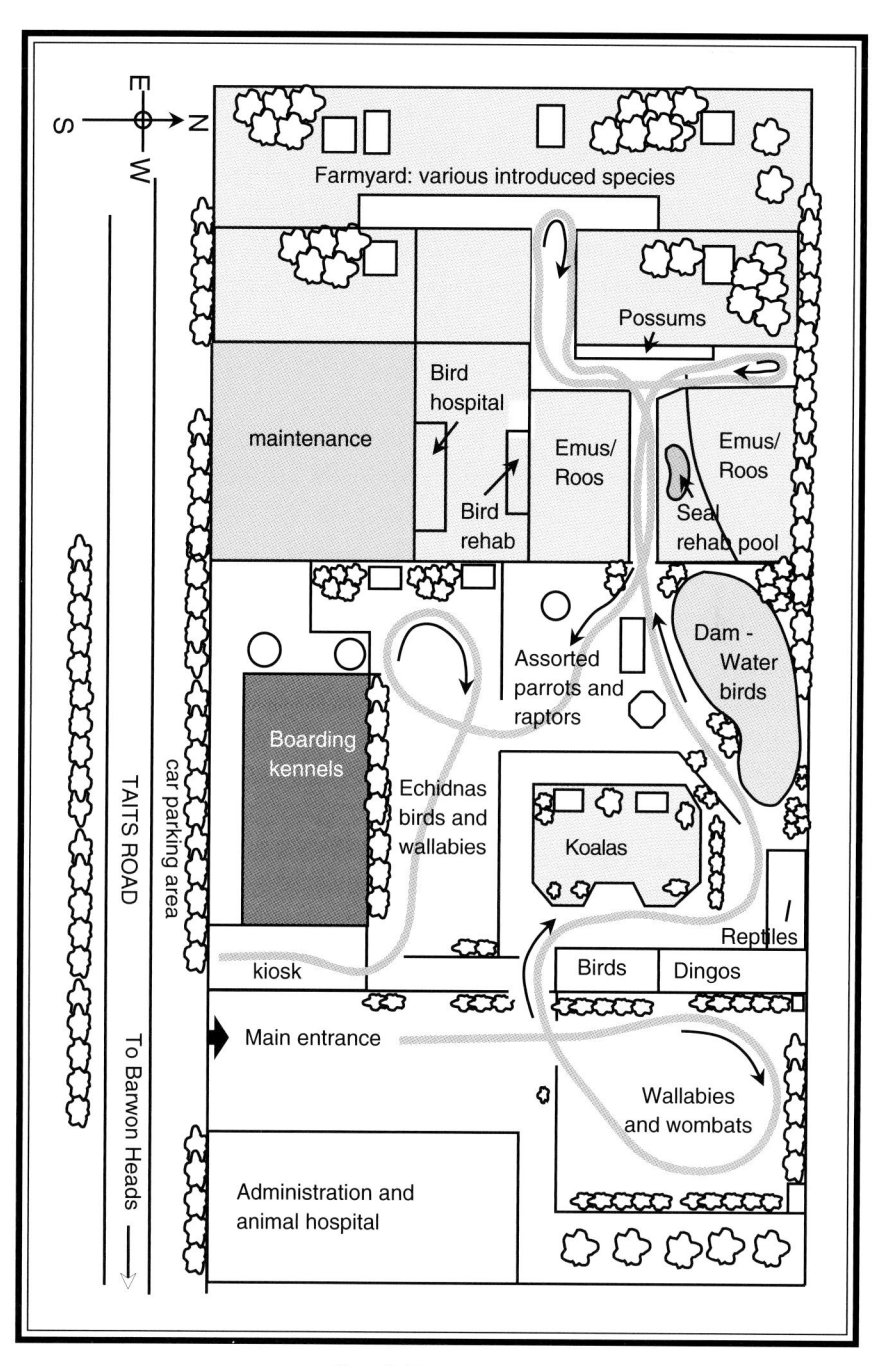

Jirrahlinga, 2002

Acknowledgements

The author and publishers would like to thank Tehree Gordon, her husband Hamish, her staff and friends, for assistance with much of the information on which this book is based.

We would also like to thank Tehree for giving us access to her photographic archive. Most of the photographs reproduced in the book were taken by her, her husband Hamish and staff, while many others were donated to them for use in publications about Jirrahlinga.

In addition, we would like to thank the following:

Craig Borrow and the Herald and Weekly Times Ltd for the front cover and for the photographs on pages 2, 78, 160, 176 and 201.

The Colac Herald for the photographs on pages 13, 93 and 97.

The Geelong Advertiser for the photograph on page 161, left.

The source of a few of the photographs in the archive is not certain, and we apologise if we have inadvertently omitted any acknowledgements from this list.

PART ONE

TEHREE

Tehree with a Redneck Wallaby rescued from the 1983 bushfires.

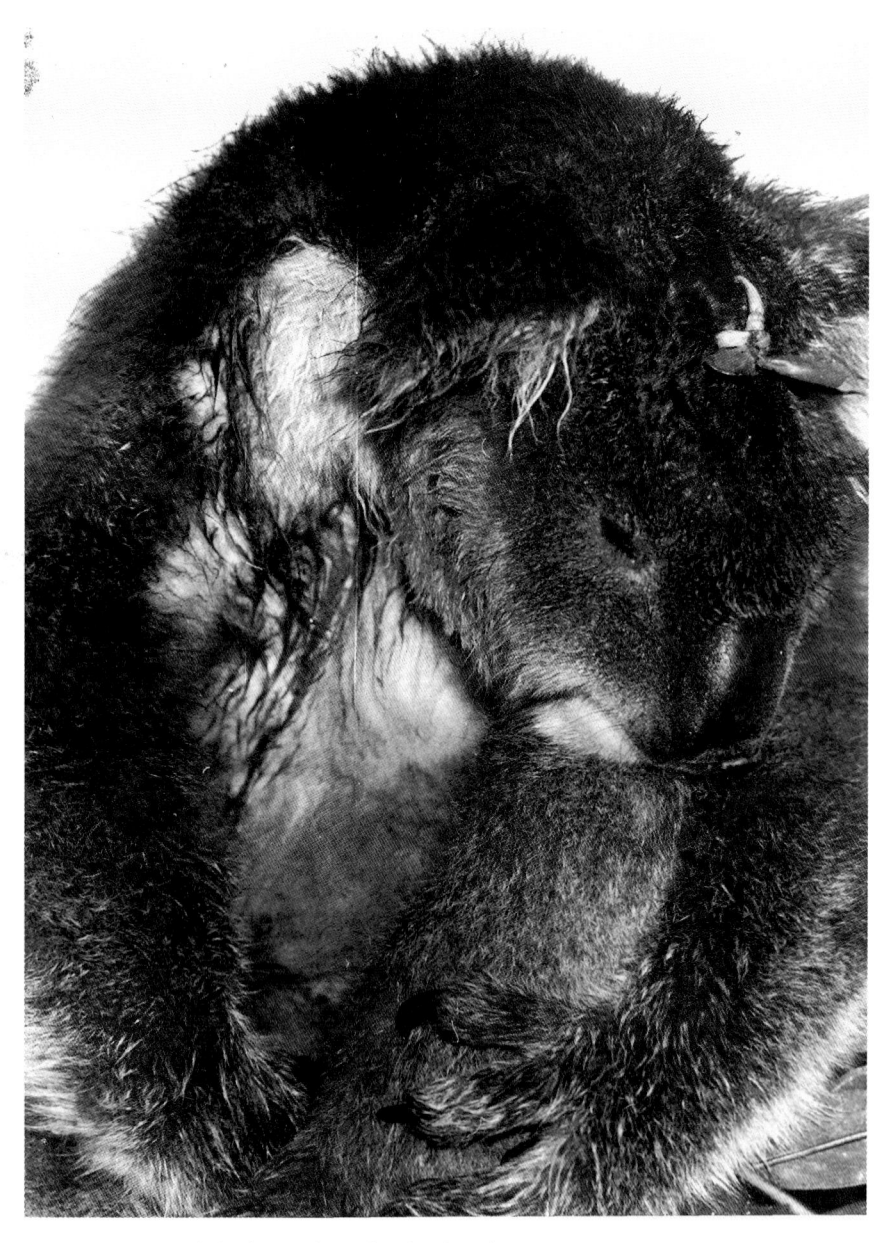

'The burned mother koala who adopted the baby.
(See pages 10–11)

1 Bushfire

THE ANCIENT BIBLICAL HELL is out of fashion these days. This may be because man has invented hells on earth so appalling that the threat of Hell in the afterlife becomes an anti-climax. Since man creates his own horrors, wars, famines, epidemics, atom bombs and all the rest he can also, to some extent, control them, but natural disasters are beyond any human control. Floods, earthquakes, blizzards and droughts make their own rules, and the firestorm stops for nothing.

The State of Victoria in Australia's south knows this demon only too well. Every few years the weather and the wind combine so that the countryside is as explosive as straw soaked in petrol, and anything from a lightning strike to a spark from a tractor can set it off. Then the wind lifts it, hunts it to the treetops and scours the ground with it, throws white-hot balls of gas ahead of it to burst and start new fires. However valiantly we fight it, we become very small indeed. A firestorm is chaos and annihilation and after it has passed there is silence, the utter quiet of ashes and death.

Ash Wednesday, 16 February 1983, was one of those catastrophic bushfire days. For Tehree Gordon, entering the bush to help rescue such wildlife as had survived the fires, the silence was extraordinary. She stood in ash, deep, black and soft, the only movement the soundless floating down of yet more ash from the blackened trees. Living bush is so full of sounds, bird-calls, animal rustlings and leaves-in-the-wind that normally you almost cease to hear them. In total silence the bush becomes surreal, nightmare territory. It stops breathing.

Almost ten years had passed since the last major fires of 1974 so that there was a build-up of dried undergrowth on the floors of the forests, while in open country the grass was at flashpoint after weeks of hot, dry weather. When these factors combine country people stay close to home, scanning the horizon for smoke and silently imploring the Gods to spare them a northerly. On Ash Wednesday the Gods turned their backs, opened the oven doors of the Central Australian deserts and let loose an overwhelming gale of red-hot air. Hardly a district in the State escaped the fires, some large, some small but all potentially disastrous in that wind. The Country Fire Authority brigades worked heroically beside fire units called from the cities, yet homes, livestock and people were incinerated. After the fires were controlled, and while a shocked Victoria rallied to the needs of humans and domestic stock, others 'went bush' to help the less widely publicised victims.

In Tehree's memory the events of Ash Wednesday started with a curious incident two days earlier, on Monday 14 February. She had gone to visit an elderly friend of hers who had a reputation for possessing second sight, not because Tehree wanted or expected clairvoyance but simply for a friendly visit and a cuppa. It was very hot, bushfire weather as everyone in the countryside knew and there's tension in such weather, especially if you have animals in your care, be it wildlife or domestic stock. Tehree's hostess suddenly stiffened, teacup held halfway to her lips, and stared at her.

'Tehree, I can see fire. It's all round you, flames everywhere.'

Tehree, already on edge and knowing her friend's reputation, froze. 'Is it Jirrahlinga? Are my animals there, can you see them?'

'Your animals are there, yes, but there's fire all round them.'

The air itself was heavy with the threat of fire and for Tehree this was confirmation of doom. She drove back to Barwon Heads at high speed, distraught and cursing herself for having left home, imagining the charred bodies of her beloved, betrayed wildlife, carnage and disaster. It was an anti-climax to find everything safe and peaceful but she was still uneasy, a pricking of the thumbs as though something monstrous was waiting, just out of sight.

The next day, Tuesday, was hotter still. Inevitably small fires were already burning in parts of the State but until Wednesday morning, when the north wind came hammering in, they were controllable. In minutes the gale had lifted the fires, spreading them through the bush and the grasslands so that the Country Fire Authority units, valiant as they were, faced impossible odds. At Jirrahlinga, as at many other places, the sky grew dark and the air thick with the smell of burning but the fire fronts were lost in the smoke; it was impossible to know whether they were far away or so close that there were only minutes left. At the Sanctuary they'd heard that the seaside town of Lorne was threatened, but at that time the wind was taking the fires south-west, away from them, and Lorne was far down the coast. They were too busy to notice when the wind changed, a sudden 180 degree shift, turning the fires and driving them headlong back eastward through the timbered Otway Ranges towards Barwon Heads. When someone came to tell them that the fires were heading their way the nightmare became real.

There's no such thing as a cool fire but some bushfires are classified as Hot, and these are the worst kind of fire. Not only do they consume utterly everything they touch but they leap ahead of themselves over the bush, fireballs carried by a combination of the wind and the fury of air which the fire itself creates. Though the fire front may be five miles away and you think you have time to escape the world can suddenly explode all round you, trapping you, as a fire ball touches down among parched trees. The fires that devastated the coast between Lorne and Torquay that year were very Hot fires indeed and the margin of safety in their path was a minus quantity. There, as in many other places on Ash Wednesday, the sudden wind shift meant that many of the fire fighting units were left on the wrong side of the fires when they changed direction.

Tehree had been burnt out before and knew about fire. The last time had been bad enough but now she had Jirrahlinga, and though she always had a plan ready for a fire emergency, its execution was no easy matter. There were, she says, about 230 assorted wild creatures, besides dogs and cats as paying boarders and a pet camel, to be moved to safety. Apart from the camel and four kangaroos, recent arrivals who were too wild still to be caught easily, the rest could be caged and transported to safety on the beach. Tehree would stay behind as long as possible to shoot the non-movable animals if the fire got very close. It would have been a hard thing to do, but anything's better than abandoning animals to fire, especially if you know animals well enough to enter their minds and feel their terror of it.

Fear, for an animal, is much worse than death, for death is natural and animals accept it as they do life. When it comes to them in the normal way they meet it with dignity, but pursuit by a predator, a human or that inescapable predator fire is menace by monsters, and they must run from it until their hearts burst or until it overtakes them. Mercifully for Jirrahlinga the wind dropped, the Otway fires were brought under control at Jan Juc, just the other side of Torquay, and Barwon Heads was untouched, though the coast from Jan Juc to Lorne was a black, smoking wasteland. In case the wind rose again, reviving the fires, Tehree and Hamish stayed up all that Wednesday night, the animals gathered into groups where they could be handled and moved quickly.

The coastline between Barwon Heads and Lorne is spectacular. Tourists drive along that coast road in raptures, clicking their cameras at the cliffs and the long, surf-fringed beaches with hardly a glance inland. For most people the view inland isn't worth a glance, just scrub, thick and monotonous, growing down to the edge of the road, sometimes to the very lip of a promontory cliff. The scrub closest to the shoreline is low and dense, flattened by the sea wind and behind it normal, upright bush rolls back over the low hills and valleys of the Otway ranges. Unless you walk through that bush you can't appreciate its complexity, its wealth of eucalypts, ferns, grasses and waterholes, a haven for kangaroos, wallabies, potoroos, koalas, possums and innumerable birds, gliders, echidnas, reptiles and a whole catalogue of lesser creatures. The blank-faced bush you see from the coast road is really a crowded container of potential bushfire victims.

Over the centuries most Australian wildlife has become genetically equipped to deal with droughts, rains, heat and cold; almost anything but fire. Their ancestors have known fire in the past, the knowledge of what the smoke and the smell of fire means is in their genes. When the smell of fire reaches them they know instinctively that their only defence is to run before it, as far and as fast as they can, until they suffocate in the smoke, or burn and die.

Most of Victoria was in damage control next day, once the fires were halted and the cost of Ash Wednesday in terms of life and property became clear. Welfare agencies, neighbours and the public in general moved quickly to help the people who had suffered, offering accommodation, donating clothes, furniture and food. Stock that had been injured were destroyed quickly and efficiently, feed provided for those that survived. Tehree and Hamish Gordon, who had just arrived back from his native Scotland, automatically moved to help the less visible victims, the wildlife in the bush.

It wasn't feasible to go into the bush that day, nor would the police allow it. There were too many hot-spots, trees and logs still smouldering and the ash underfoot not yet cooled. As soon as the fires started on Ash Wednesday Tehree had called the police to say that Jirrahlinga would house domestic animals belonging to the people who had been burned out, free of charge. On Thursday she rang the police again to ask them to direct anyone with injured animals of any kind to Jirrahlinga, and on Friday she started to organise the wildlife rescue which lasted until a week after Easter and became, for her, an all-consuming mission.

'We went to see the police at Anglesea,' she remembers. 'They said we could go along the main roads but not into the bush yet. We had food and water with us for the animals but we didn't know then the best way to go about getting it to them. We didn't know what we were going to find, really. It was weird just driving along the road because everything was black, nothing but black and only the road was pale, like a ribbon through it. Every now and then there'd be a little patch of bush that the fires had missed, just as it'd miss one house and burn others alongside it, and those live patches were strange too, in all the black.

'There were kangaroos, still panicked and running. They'd dash out of the bush across the road towards the sea, then hit the hot ash on the other side and turn back. There were other cars about, official ones, and we saw four 'roos hit in about twenty minutes so we stopped and put some water containers down, back from the road on the inland side. More 'roos came, but we saw that they slowed down when they got the smell of the water and didn't try to cross the road. We got home about midnight but at least we had some idea about how to help them.'

The next day they went out with two vehicles loaded with water, water containers and food, grasses, fruit and vegetables, anything they could lay hands on that wildlife might eat. Peters Ice Cream had donated a mass of plastic ice cream cartons which they numbered so that they could be sure of collecting them all again. They filled these with water and placed them and the food back from the road, where the animals could smell them and find them. Until after Easter, a period of some weeks, Tehree and her volunteers refilled the water containers and replaced the food twice every twenty-four hours, covering the whole area between Torquay and Lorne. In the course of this they collected as many injured creatures as they could, taking them back to Jirrahlinga for treatment and eventual rehabilitation.

The rescue was organised in conjunction with the police, the Barrabool Shire and the Conservation Department, the Government body that has now become the Department of Natural Resources and Environment, and one of the Jirrahlinga staff stayed at the police station to oversee the volunteers. A great many people offered to help, but before they were allowed to go into the fire area they had to register their driving licenses and license plate numbers at the police station checkpoint. They were also asked to establish that they had no physical disability that might turn them into additional casualties. Two licensed drivers had to be in each car and their time of departure and estimated time of return documented, partly, but not entirely, for their own protection. The checks had a twofold purpose for as well as the possibility of well-meaning volunteers becoming lost or being injured there was the danger of looters, aiming for the empty and unprotected properties in the fire zone. Tehree was anxious that if looting did take place there should be no possibility that it was done under the blanket of helping in the animal rescue. It's an interesting sidelight on this that a third of the volunteers withdrew their offers of help when they were told of the checks which would be applied to them.

In the early days the rescue team had to learn by trial and error the best way to help the survivors. Tehree said, 'We'd put food and water out beside the road and then go back a bit to watch what happened. The animals would be waiting for it because they soon got used to us coming, and we saw that the badly injured ones were always the last to come out. We could catch some of those, and that was traumatic too. Often you knew you were catching them just to put them down, the ones with terrible burns and broken limbs or blinded. We had to judge which to catch because chasing and handling adult 'roos for instance would have caused them terrible stress, and it was better for them if we could help them to recover on their own.'

'There was a huge grey kangaroo, a buck, we saw on the road and he came to be a sort of symbol to us because he really wanted to survive. He was very badly burned and he had a big gash on the side of his head where something had hit him. You couldn't have caught him, firstly because he could have killed you and second because the trauma of being caught would have been worse to him than dying, but he was a very sick kangaroo. We put food and water out for him every day because he never moved from the same little clump of scrub that the fire had missed, and every day he'd be there waiting for us.'

'I got a vet to put antibiotics into some apples and we'd put these out before the main food so that he'd eat them. He'd be standing by his dish waiting for us every night, and he'd growl at us to warn us

Wallabies with burned feet in care after the bushfires.

not to come too close but he wouldn't run away. We gradually moved his food back from the road into the bush; we did this with all the food so that the animals would get back into their natural habitat and away from the traffic. Anyway, this big old buck gradually got better and in the end he moved right back to a property that hadn't been burned. He lived there for years, you could always tell it was him by the scar on his head. He had an amazing will to live, so many of the animals had that determination to survive. You felt you just had to help them.'

There were others that died although their injuries were minor. Stress, with wildlife, is one of the greatest killers and these were creatures who had been through unendurable stress. Others, with severe injuries, survived because of their unconquerable determination to do so. No-one, not even Tehree who fought to rescue, nurse and rehabilitate burned, injured and traumatised wild creatures during those weeks, can fully understand that will to live. It can't be explained in humans either, that inner spirit which refuses to surrender, and even the people who possess such strength haven't the words to explain it. There were triumphs when an animal fought to live and won, together with utter helplessness when another dropped its head, sank into the death-sleep and gave up.

'Some died of stress, and that was understandable, but you couldn't always tell from the external injuries what would live and what wouldn't,' Tehree told me. ' Some of the ones that had been badly burned or had terrible cuts and broken bones did well with treatment, but others without a mark on them unaccountably died. This puzzled us until the vets did a post mortem on one of these mystery deaths and after that we knew what was wrong. Even though they'd escaped the fire they'd breathed in air so hot that their insides looked as though they'd been microwaved, just cooked solid. There was no way they could have lived. I could often tell in the end, just by holding them, which we could save and which was on the way out.

'There were wonderful things that happened too. If there hadn't been we couldn't have stood it. There was a female koala with a little cub. He had pneumonia and she was in such a bad way we knew we'd have to put her down so we took the baby away while we did it and it was in a basket, crying for its mum. There was another female across the room with badly burned ears and paws and you wouldn't have blamed her for giving up the battle. We were thinking she might have to be put down too but she heard the cub crying, called to it and allowed it to crawl to her and climb onto her tummy. She fought us when we tried to take it away so we left them together. She had this amazing will to live. They stayed together and in time they both recovered but I don't believe either of them would have survived on their own. They gave each other something to live for.'

Human reactions to the rescue effort were varied and at times unaccountable. On one side were the volunteer helpers; vets, ordinary residents, students and pensioners who did whatever they could, and without them only a fraction of the wildlife could have been saved. There were some who brought food for the animals. The owner of a small garage in Highton lent a truck to help in food distribution and filled it with petrol every week. Tehree says, with infinite gratitude, that her volunteers were a random selection of ordinary and extraordinary people who understood the agony in the bush, and cared.

On the other side were those incomprehensible characters who invariably manage to sour the milk of human kindness, having none of their own. 'What's the use of spending time and money saving an animal?' they asked Tehree, as if this was some stupid, publicity-grabbing eccentricity. 'Give it to people, they're the ones who need it.' Every welfare organisation in the State, the Government and the public were in fact, and quite rightly, helping the human bushfire victims but the wildlife were not so lucky.

It took some days for many of the animals to emerge from whatever shelter they'd been able to find. During those days they cowered in terror of the world outside, still traumatised, hurting and hungry. Quite early on, while the surviving animals were at their most desperate, and the rescuers were struggling to get supplies of suitable feed a local landholder confronted Tehree, hot with indignation.

'That grass you're putting out everywhere for the bloody animals,' he said. 'It's not the local grass, you know. What d'you think it's going to do to my land when it seeds here? If you're going to put out grass it's got to be local grass.'

Tehree, who might have agreed with him in normal circumstances, surveyed the black, scorched earth around them and said, 'Where do you suggest I find local grass? You bring it to me in a truck and I'll put it out, but until then these animals have to be fed.'

The ecologically pure objected to the ice-cream containers full of water, the thing that the survivors craved and needed most of all. 'You'll never remember to pick all those plastic things up,' they said. 'They're not biodegradable you know, they'll be there forever spoiling our bush.'

'They're all numbered according to the area they're in and the areas are numbered too. We know how many are out and where they are. We check them twice every day to see how much water has been drunk and refill them. We'll pick them all up when they're not needed any more.'

On the other hand there were people like the owner of a house which had been almost totally destroyed. The rescuers had discovered that under what was left of the house there were three terrified and badly singed little potoroos, an attractive and harmless species of marsupial, taking shelter in the only secure place they could find. The rescue team put food and water beside the wreckage and let them be, knowing that with time and nourishment they'd survive. They were delivering the potoroos' rations when the householder arrived to view what was left of his house and consider restoring it. When Tehree explained to him that the burnt-out shell was now home to three refugees he said, 'Let them have it then. It's only a holiday house and I won't be holidaying here for a while. I'll forget about cleaning the place up; the little beggars can have it as long as they need it.'

Before long Jirrahlinga was like a field hospital after a major battle. Casualties far outnumbered the existing animal accommodation, the nursery and the hospital were packed with the worst cases and the

A DNRE officer with a kookaburra nursed back to health at Jirrahlinga and ready for release.

overflow was being housed in Tehree and Hamish's small cottage. Cages and pouches filled every room and the worst thing of all was the smell. Not so much the smell of animal excreta, though inevitably there was that too, but the reek of burnt animals, burnt hair, burnt flesh and trauma, for fear has a smell of its own. Even though all the windows were wide open there was no escaping that smell. It clung to people too and Tehree said they couldn't wash it off.

There was little time for food and less for sleep. Most of the rescue work had to be done at night because everything, landscape and animals alike, was the colour of charcoal. An injured animal was invisible in daylight unless it moved, but at night with a spotlight they could find them by the glint of their eyes, and check on them to see if they were fully mobile or in need of help. Many of the koalas and possums had badly burned paws, and almost all of the animals had eyes affected by smoke and heat. Paws and eyes could be treated and cured at Jirrahlinga and the animals could be fed, but possums and koalas, unable to climb trees for food and left to themselves, must starve.

The rescue teams would set out in the evening and drive back to Jirrahlinga in the small hours, the vehicles empty of feed and water but loaded with new patients. Then the first aid would begin, and the ongoing treatment of earlier casualties never stopped. Strangers arrived at all hours with more hurt and dying creatures to be housed and bandaged and fed. Jirrahlinga bulged and threatened to burst at the seams, its owner and her helpers were sleepwalking, too tired to be conscious of anything except their compulsion to save whatever could be saved. Even the sea along the coast was a graveyard. Kangaroos and wallabies, being natural flight animals unlike possums and koalas, had run for their lives in front of the fires. Some had been trapped, some injured and many, confused by the smoke, the heat and the fear had simply hurtled over the headland cliffs into the sea. The water off these headlands was full of bodies, bloated and floating. Underwater scavengers would welcome the carcases, and perhaps death by drowning had been easier than death by fire.

Tehree told me of one particular incident that somehow symbolised the fires for her, the heat, the horror and their awful power to overwhelm everything in their path.

'For some reason there was one special thing,' she said. 'It stayed with me and haunted me and I don't know quite why it should have been that particular one. A friend of mine and I were in the bush soon after the fires, looking for hurt animals. The ash was so deep it came up to our shins, it made walking very hard but you could see animal tracks in it and we were following a koala track. I stumbled over what looked like a great black log and at the same time Eileen called out, "I can see her, she's over here," but when we found her she was dead.

'It was when we were walking back through the ash that I saw the black log again. I stopped and looked at it and I said to Eileen, "I nearly fell flat on my face over this just before you called out to me." Then suddenly I saw that it wasn't a log at all, it was a horse. It was stretched out in full gallop as it must have been when the smoke finally choked it and it just fell. Then the fire went over it. There were little rivers of steel running from its feet where its shoes had melted.

'For some reason that horse got to me. The thought of it galloping in front of the fire till it dropped wouldn't leave me alone, I could feel its terror. I walked along the beach and cried about it and one night I dreamed about it. In my dream it was a grey horse. After all the rescue work was over I went back and asked the local people if anyone around there had lost a grey horse in the fires. They said two horses had been lost and one of them was grey. I still couldn't tell you why it was so important, but in some way that horse said everything I felt about those fires.'

It is easy to see how the Tawny Frogmouth, or Mopoke, is the camouflage champion among Australian birds. It looks like the dead limb of a tree even in close-up

2   Tehree's Jirrahlinga

WHEN I FIRST MET Tehree Gordon I knew almost nothing about her, or about her Wildlife Sanctuary, Jirrahlinga. The little I knew I'd learned from Ninon Phillips, a brilliant wildlife artist and an animal carer . She advised me to take a young Eastern Grey kangaroo to Jirrahlinga for halfway-housing, the essential period of transition from human hand-raising to release into the bush. I rang Tehree and she gave me directions. I thought I knew Barwon Heads quite well but nobody there had ever mentioned Jirrahlinga to me.

Barwon Heads, the small seaside town where the Barwon River meets the sea, is not a place one would readily associate with a Wildlife Sanctuary. Its reputation is for its golf course, its elite Golf Club and for the age and affluence of its residents, rather than for dedicated wildlife ventures. Graziers, lawyers, industrialists and the like, or more frequently their widows, retire there to play golf or bridge, gossip and share their evening intake of alcoholic stimulant. Barwon Heads has been referred to unkindly as God's Waiting Room, but at least the waiting is done convivially and in comfort.

The road from Geelong runs through the sandy, flat country of the Bellarine Peninsula, the ocean coast on your right, Port Phillip Bay on the left, arriving in Barwon Heads almost without warning. One moment there's a straight, rural road, the next a service station, a roundabout, and on your right you're aware of many houses, insulated from each other by protective trees. Barwon Heads cherishes and respects privacy, even though the proximity of its houses would rival that of suburban Melbourne. If you turn left instead of right at the roundabout you're in what amounts to the Wrong Side of the Barwon Heads Tracks and the elite, who live at the Paris End near the Golf Club or on the river, will be less than aware of you. Another left turn, not far from the first, will lead you to Jirrahlinga.

When I first saw it in the early 1980s Jirrahlinga was in the middle stage of its development. At the top end there was a small weatherboard house, boarding kennels for dogs and below that a few sheds.

There were small paddocks full of kangaroos of varying ages, smaller enclosures for wombats and koalas and larger paddocks inhabited by a mixture of sheep, goats, ponies and one camel. There were birdcages and the chatter of bird voices, dominated by the shrieking of white cockatoos. It was functional and diverse but without trimmings, the fencing of the various enclosures secure but by no means fancy. The eastern side of the main road in those days was hardly inhabited, apart from the river's edge, and in contrast to the treed, manicured gardens of the Paris End of Barwon Heads it was swampy, unappealing country. A tall hedge separated Jirrahlinga from a rough gravel road and the paddocks beyond the road had the scrawny look of land not highly valued.

The first impression I had of Tehree, when I ran her to earth cleaning out a cage, was entirely correct because I identified her at once as a hard worker, even though I had no idea then that the term 'hard worker' was totally inadequate. If you work with animals of any kind they and their by-products rub off on you, and that is as it should be. If an employee on our thoroughbred stud looked clean at the end of the day I knew he or she wouldn't last long with us. Tehree was in gumboots, appropriately grubby, with her sleeves rolled up and hair tousled. She had a set to her jaw fit for a sergeant major and light brown eyes that were unusually direct, weighing me up as good, bad or indifferent. It crossed my mind that I wouldn't like to get on the wrong side of Tehree and at the same moment, instinctively, that I liked her very much. She agreed to halfway-house the little 'roo for me, then offered to show me round Jirrahlinga while we waited for him to settle in.

We went to the nursery, a shed with a humidicrib and cages of every size and shape, some occupied by birds and others by koalas, baby 'roos and wombats, the older ones climbing in and out of their cloth pouches. Three tiny echidnas stood up against the wire of their cage, tummies pink and smooth, beaks twitching, curious as young puppies. The food that lay on the cage floors, fruit, lettuce leaves and eucalyptus branches in the koala cages was all fresh and the place smelled as antiseptically clean as a well kept ward in a hospital. The smaller animals would all need regular bottle feeding, the birds anything from meat to seeds or insects and the amount of work involved in maintaining this shed alone was awesome, without the additional variety of wildlife in cages and enclosures outside.

It was beginning to dawn on me that the woman who ran this operation was no ordinary woman, even though I didn't know then the story of the bushfires. I asked her, 'How long have you had this place? How did you start?'

'I bought five acres down here in the seventies. It wasn't the land I wanted; there was a place right on the coast overlooking the sea, but the deal fell through and I bought this. It's five acres altogether and I already had a Shelter Permit, so when the animals and so forth started coming it soon filled up. I came down here first with a dog, a gun, a tent and a kangaroo with a broken leg. The house was still being lived in when I came, so I slept in one of the sheds and I've been here ever since. We're still sort of growing and I've got lots of plans for Jirrahlinga, if we can ever afford to carry them out.'

'I slept in one of the sheds and I've been here ever since.' Jirrahlinga c. 1985.

'But how did you manage to build the nursery and all the rest of it? Did you get any special funding?'

'Not official funding; Wildlife Shelters don't get any as you'd know because you've got a Shelter yourself, but people come and see what we're doing and give us donations. I work as a Shire Ranger during the day and for a caterer at night, and Hamish, my husband, has his job as well. We manage somehow but it's been a battle and we always need more money than we can get. Some of the animals we've got here are still bushfire victims who'll never be fit for release, or others who've been too badly hurt or too humanised to go back to the bush, and they'll stay here always. Everything that can be released will go when it's ready, but new ones just keep on coming. We've got a bit of name for ourselves now and I never turn anything away. If it's something that has to be put down we do it here rather than risk it being done badly.'

'It must be one hell of a struggle without proper funding. What keeps you going, Tehree?'

She was silent for a few moments, then said, 'I know it sounds silly but I really believe I'm meant to look after animals, it's like having a vocation of some sort. I didn't have much of a childhood and animals have always meant a lot to me, not just wildlife but all animals because they accept me exactly as I am. I like people too, but animals seem to me to get less help than people do. I'll try to explain it all to you some day, if you're interested.'

'How about helpers? You can't possibly do all this single handed.'

'We can't afford paid staff yet but we have volunteers. Then there's what I call our Special People. Some of them are really good when they've been here a while.'

'Special People? What d'you mean?'

'People who for some reason or another are in care – abused kids, delinquents and the intellectually disabled, people like that. We work in with the Salvos and other organisations and it's amazing how being with animals helps these people. The intellectually disabled come on visits with their carers, and some of them even do simple jobs while they are here. The others, with all kinds of problems, work with the staff and sometimes stay in the house with Hamish and me. It's great to see how they improve.'

All this was told to me quite casually, understated if anything, and it gave me a great deal to think about on the way home, but it was to be some years before I heard Tehree's story properly. My husband had died, I was forced to sell Willowmavin Stud and move to Melbourne, and a Wildlife Shelter in a tiny suburban garden was clearly impossible. Before I cancelled my Wildlife Shelter permit I'd been to Jirrahlinga a number of times with young kangaroos or wombats, but never with enough time or a valid reason to learn much about Tehree. I sensed though that she had a gift, both with animals and with people, and enormous dedication.

Then we met again. I'd just published a book and Tehree came to a talk I gave at Warrnambool, a seaside town on Victoria's south coast. I was overjoyed to see her, but surprised that she remembered me well enough to drive all that way to see me. I called in at Jirrahlinga on the way back to Melbourne and found it had been transformed from the professional but unadorned Shelter I remembered into as complex and attractive a Wildlife Sanctuary as I've ever seen. There were new buildings, a smart entrance with a kiosk just inside it where visitors could have tea or coffee and buy souvenirs, opposite that a door labelled 'Hospital' and a small office building. Two large, new aviaries housed a variety of birds, golden pheasants, plovers and rosellas exchanging gossip while from beyond a security fence, separating the main sanctuary from the entrance, came the unmistakable racket of cockatoos. Mixed with the bird voices were dog voices, these coming from the brand-new boarding kennels, and the occasional basso profundo honk of Cape Barren geese. An elderly kangaroo dozed placidly on the grass and a mother swan, full of self-importance, paraded her cygnets nearby.

The rough fences were a thing of the past and in their place were neat mud walls, or for the koala enclosure Colorbond fencing, impossible for the koalas to climb. Clean raked paths bordered with flower beds led round kangaroo and wallaby enclosures and in smaller, secure wombat homes with straw-lined hollow logs for daytime sleeping, the round, hairy backsides of the occupants pointed outward to block the light. Nothing sleeps with greater determination than a grown wombat, and being woken from a daytime sleep constitutes a gross insult. Beyond the wombats, heated reptile tanks had appeared, the resident pythons warm and somnolent as such snakes should be in a cold climate. Further down the Sanctuary was a cyclone fence round a swimming pool for the seals and penguins and more cyclone cages, tall ones for the flight of raptors and smaller ones where possums slept or cockatoos shouted for attention.

Trees had grown up everywhere, young trees planted to shade the cages and enclosures in summer heat and beneath them Tehree's staff, including a couple of identifiably Special People, were busy in smart green and fawn Jirrahlinga uniforms. As well as the animal hospital near the entrance there was a separate special building for koalas, sick, injured or in need of care. Altogether it was like meeting a smart, affluent, handsome young man whom you'd last seen as a small boy with his shirt tails hanging out. I kept saying, 'My God, Tehree, how have you done all this?' and she looked puzzled, as if she didn't understand why I was so excited.

'I don't notice the change so much myself,' she said, looking round. 'It sort of just happened, like the trees. You plant them and then suddenly they're grown but you haven't really been conscious of them growing.'

'Did the Department give you some funding at last? All this must have cost money.'

'No, we still don't get anything from the Government but we can charge for people to come in here now, and we get some donations. Hamish's job helps and we have volunteer workers as well as six paid staff and our Special People. We never have enough money to do what we want with the place, but every cent we make goes back into it and things get done gradually, when we have a bit of spare cash.'

In 1975 when Tehree arrived on her newly bought five acres with 'a tent, a dog, a gun and a kangaroo with a broken leg;' she could hardly have imagined what the place would eventually become. If someone had warned her then of the complexities and problems in her future she might well have decided to develop a market garden instead of a sanctuary. The fact that in spite of the odds against her, ill-health, lack of funding, staff problems and daily animal crises she has stuck to Jirrahlinga is proof enough of her 'vocation'. Money must be found for salaries, for the multiple foodstuffs and supplements, medications, repairs, maintenance, transport and the building of new wildlife accommodation.

Tehree's estimate of the annual cost of running Jirrahlinga is about $200,000. Of this about 15% comes from gate money, 15% from donations and the rest from Hamish's job and the work Tehree does with her wildlife exhibits at functions and conferences, and their appearances in films. Donations can't be counted on with any certainty, neither can a steady supply of film work or bookings for wildlife exhibits, and unexpected expenses can mean near financial disaster.

Their worst period came after the Ash Wednesday bushfires, during which Tehree and Hamish had spent great deal of their own money. When something was urgently needed for the animals there was no time to appeal for donors, nor was there time to add up what they were spending. In the eyes of the Government caring for wildlife should be a labour of love, but in the wake of Ash Wednesday love had to be accompanied by expensive, specialised foods and supplements, medical supplies, petrol for the feed-and-water vehicles, food for the volunteers and a hundred other daily items. There were donations and volunteer help, there was public sympathy and media publicity but the money still went out much faster than it came in. At one time there were more than 600 individual patients at Jirrahlinga, all receiving treatment and care.

When Tehree and Hamish had time to look at their finances they found they were within an inch of bankruptcy. They approached the Government with records and invoices and asked for some form of restitution, having done a job that could never have been achieved by the then Conservation Department's slender resources alone. They were told by the Labour Government then in power that their losses would be made up to them, and they felt a little easier. Before this could happen the Government changed and the incoming Liberal Government turned their backs on the claim. In the end, under pressure, they were repaid a small portion, described as an ex gratia payment. The truth was that the Gordons and their volunteer helpers had saved the Government and the State a great deal of money, besides rescuing invaluable wildlife.

Situations such as the influx during the Ash Wednesday fires luckily occur very seldom, whereas the everyday running of Jirrahlinga must stay within a budget and Tehree has learned to be pragmatic in terms of time, money and labour. If her philosophy of universal care were taken to extremes her Sanctuary would be a financial disaster, swamped with inmates. This means that hard decisions must often be made on what wildlife to take into care, what to treat and what to put down. Creatures hand-raised or recovered from injury or sickness are always released, those who are unsuitable for release are kept as exhibits, in company with a few exotic specimens such as snakes as part of the Sanctuary's attractions. Jirrahlinga's population fluctuates with new arrivals and departures, but they all have to be fed.

Budget restrictions also mean that staff must be kept to an affordable minimum, learn to abandon strictly 'nine-to-five' expectations and to cope with crises when they arise. Volunteers are invaluable because they do their work purely for their love of the wildlife, and every hour they spend at Jirrahlinga is a financial bonus.

Most of the people who care for Australia's wildlife, apart from the Shelters and sympathetic vets, expect some form of monetary return. Most good vets treat wildlife free of charge but they, after all, have an alternative income. Jirrahlinga, created from nothing, without official funding and perpetually short of money, was clearly the product of sheer dedication and I wanted to know more about its creator. With some diffidence I suggested I might write about Tehree and her Sanctuary. I said, 'It'll probably drive you mad. I'll want to know about your childhood, why you're so hooked on wildlife, your jobs, stories about the animals, everything. Can you be bothered?'

'If you think it's worth writing about of course I can.' Then she told me that she'd recently been diagnosed as having Multiple Sclerosis and that she'd also had a stroke. 'I have good days and bad days,' she said. 'But this'll be fun, it'll bring a lot of things back that I've half-forgotten.'

3   Growing Up

By most accepted standards Tehree's childhood seems to have been on the horrifying side of merely awful. She doesn't indulge in self-pity, but even so it's one of the few things, other than animal disasters, that she's unable to laugh about. It's still visible in her mind, and to hear her tell it one can understand very well why animals became more important to her than people. A childhood like Tehree's is a mountainous thing to overcome. There's no Road-to-Damascus moment when it stops being important; it's as much part of you as your skin or your guts, and you have to get a long distance from it before you can see it dispassionately. Even then its ghost hovers in the background, making you doubt your own achievements because you've been told so often, by your own father, that you could never achieve anything worthwhile.

Tehree was the eldest of four children; the second child, a boy, was born five years later. Her father was descended from a Catholic family which traditionally gave its eldest son, and the eldest child was always a boy, to the Church. It seems that he had counted obsessively on doing this too, presumably in expiation for his own character which was a combination of sadism, hypocrisy and criminal irresponsibility. Confronted with a girl child, who could not hope to score the necessary number of celestial Brownie points for him, he proceeded to make her life a misery, to punish her for being a girl. The other children were to suffer in their turn, without the excuse of gender but simply as victims of his personality. Their gallant, long-suffering mother probably had the worst time of all, since she had to try to defend her young and at the same time provide a semblance of family life.

Her father was a drifter, the master of a long list of manual skills but unable to settle to any of them so that the family was always on the move, a job in a town, a job on a property, then to another State in search of something different. One week there'd be money to buy some food, the next they'd be living in a tent with no money at all, always with the threat of a beating if they moved or spoke out of line. Tehree says she went to twenty-nine different primary schools. Each time they shifted she'd come out with her school books to put them in the car and her father would snatch them from her and tear them up. Her mother brought them out for her on one occasion and still he threw them away. Tehree was no use to anyone, he told her, no good, a burden that should never have happened.

A child who's always on the move doesn't make friends, or if she does they're gone before they've had time to become proper friends. For this reason alone it was natural for Tehree to turn to animals for company. She was convinced that she was as worthless as her father continually said she was and infinitely grateful that animals accepted her, even appeared to like her. She acquired a puppy. It doesn't take much imagination to see what a puppy must have meant to a child like Tehree; the Holy Grail would have seemed a mere bauble beside it. Her father picked her up from school one day in the car to drive her home. Her puppy ran from the house to meet her and he deliberately ran over it, either to show his dominance or to punish her for existing.

Tehree's gift with animals, of empathy and communication with them on a quite inexplicable level, was starting to emerge even then. When she was very small they'd lived near a cousin who was involved in racing and who would often put her on a horse and give her a ride, a certain recipe for enchantment in a little girl, and later on, among their constant moves, she came across horses again. The property they were on was a big enough place to keep a sizeable mob of stock horses which ran loose, until they were needed for mustering when they'd be rounded up and yarded by the stockmen. Horses who live like that are a flighty lot, ready to use their teeth or their hooves because they have no reason at all to love the human race or to welcome its approach. Tehree's school bus passed their range and one evening she was unaccountably late home.

'Where the hell have you been?' her father asked when she came in.

Tehree was on too much of a high to be cautious. 'Talking to the horses,' she said.

'Yeah? And I suppose they talked back.'

'Yes; they did, they talked to me.'

A savage clip to her head sent her flying. 'Don't you ever dare tell me horses talk. Get into your room and stay there! No tea for you when you tell lies like that.'

Her mother brought her food later on but the argument continued. Every evening her father would say, 'Are you going to admit you lied? Will you stop saying horses can talk?' Each time the child would say stubbornly, 'But they do, they talk to me,' and get smacked and sent to bed. It ended only when her mother stepped in front of her husband one evening and said, 'Stop it! She's right, they do talk to her, I've seen it.'

She had gone secretly to watch, where the bus stopped near the big horse paddock, watched Tehree get out and run to the fence where she climbed onto a strainer post. There were no horses to be seen but the child started shouting and making whinnying noises, 'Come on, come on, I'm here!' Suddenly there was the sound of horses' hooves and over the brow of a hill came the mob. Tehree jumped down from her post and ran towards them, laughing and calling to them, then walked among them, touching, kissing, talking and the half-wild beasts nuzzled and followed her, gentle as pet dogs.

There are many stories of horses and children, their recognition of something very young and their protectiveness towards it. I've seen it myself, even in stallions who were dangerous with an adult yet would let a child walk between their legs. To a child like Tehree, whose affinity with animals was part of her and who had so little else in her life, the friendship of the horses must have been like suddenly finding she had wings.

Her magic with the stock horses became known. The Boss came to their cottage one evening and asked for her.

'The men can't get the horses in,' he said, 'and they're needed for a muster in the morning. Could your daughter come and get them for us, d'you think?'

She went and called them and they came in a jostling, trusting bunch and the stockmen yarded them. There was nothing her father could say then because the Boss had asked her to call them.

It was on this property that she first had Aboriginal friends. 'I went to school and that's where I met Aboriginal kids. I thought they were the smartest kids on earth because they knew about the land and rain and all the animals and I wanted to be like them, black, because then I'd know those things too.

'James was my special friend; he taught me all sorts of things and I made him laugh all the time because I was "silly white fella" when it came to things like tracking or riding, and he beat me hollow at hid-and-seek. He could do all the things I liked doing better than I could and I got to walking behind him all the time, hoping I'd turn the same black colour as him, thinking that then I'd be the same. My mother asked me why I always walked behind him so I told her. She said, "Friends ought to walk together even if they're different, and for goodness sake don't tell your father you want to be black." I realised that made sense even though I didn't understand why.'

To hear Tehree talk of her mother it's impossible not to believe that much as she loved and tried to protect her children she still loved her husband, and that in his distorted way he cared for her. She was the one safe harbour for the children in the tempest he created. Probably, although he maltreated, neglected and abused her, perpetually letting her down, she was his only link with a semblance of stability and reason. Tehree has a story about one of her brothers, asked by their mother to do something for her, saying 'What?' either because he hadn't heard her or wasn't paying attention. His father hit him so hard that he flew across the table and landed on the floor on the other side.

'What! Don't you ever say "what" to your mother again or I'll kill you!' It was violent and ugly, but arguably to defend his wife against a breach of manners. According to Tehree she never heard her mother run her father down, although she did her best to protect the children and to make up for his violence. While he spent his wages on drink and cigarettes and gambling she made do with what little money was left. In all the stories Tehree has told me about her childhood there isn't one that involves an outright quarrel between her parents so that somehow, in spite of everything, there must have been affection between them.

When Tehree was about eight years old her father took a job on a property outside Broken Hill. The children, the youngest then a baby, went up by train with their mother to join him and Tehree remembers seeing her first inland sunrise from the train window, painting

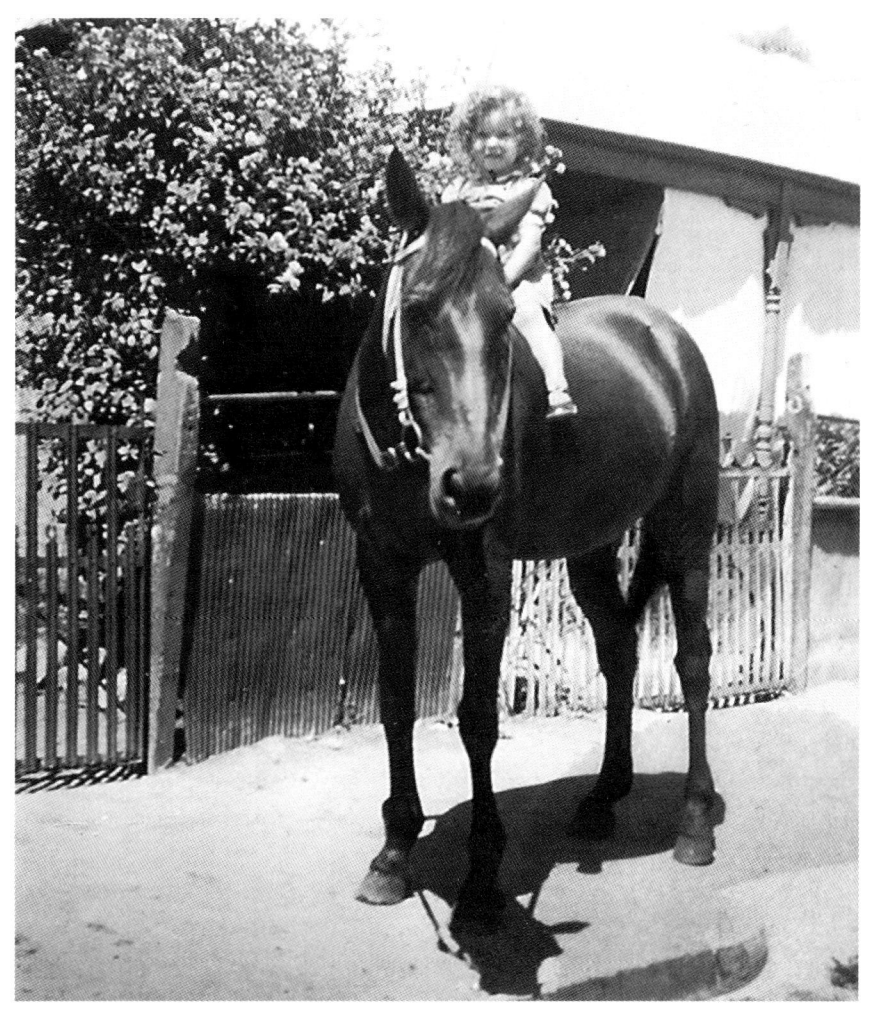

Tehree with friend. Her extraordinary capacity to communicate with animals became evident at an early age.

gold a string of great red kangaroos, her first red kangaroos, keeping pace with the train. When they arrived in Broken Hill, her mother saddled with four dog-tired and dusty children, their father was not there to meet them.

    He finally appeared to pick them up. 'We drove and drove until we arrived at a dry, bare hillside with two tents on it, and that's where we lived. He brought us three rubbish bins of water once a week and that's all the water we had. We kids found a goat and we took it back to the tents. Mother asked what it was going to drink and said that if it drank our water there'd be less for us because there wouldn't be enough to go round. If we wanted the goat to stay we had to go without, that's what sharing means, she said. We gave the goat our water at first but we were so thirsty ourselves that we couldn't keep it for long. We wanted to, but there wasn't enough water for all of us and we had to take it back to its herd. We felt guilty because we hadn't been able to share.'

Their mother couldn't drive, even if there had been a car other than the one her husband used all the time, so as well as their primitive living conditions they existed in total isolation. Finally she could stand it no longer, and they quit the hillside and the three bins of water, moving the tents into a disused shearing shed. Then someone lent them an old caravan and life improved.

There was a lengthy period when the children were separated from their parents; Tehree says they were never told the reason. 'A trauma of some sort,' she says. 'Everyone was very quiet, but we were never told what it was about.' She and her sister were sent to a Christian Welfare establishment for children in crisis. They were there for some time, long enough for her to become established at a proper school called Haddon House. She was assessed on arrival and declared that she intended to be a vet because already she felt instinctively that her future lay with animals. To become a vet was a simple, logical choice but the response came as a shock.

'Not possible,' said her assessor. 'You've done none of the subjects you need for that but you can try for a scholarship if you like.' She failed miserably the first time, but the second time she tried to qualify to sit for the scholarship she got almost full marks and could dream of actually achieving a degree in Veterinary Science. She enjoyed learning, loved the stability of school and the Welfare Home. 'No violence,' she says. 'No shouting and belting and belittling.'

Predictably her father turned up again two weeks before she was to sit for the scholarship, collected her and her sister and swept his family off to Keith in South Australia. To leave Tehree in no doubt that she was back under his thumb again, he burned her books. 'You will never, ever,' he told her as he did so, 'be a vet.' It wasn't so much a dislike of animals as jealousy of his daughter's devotion to them, a love that he felt should have been given to him.

In Keith they lived in a stone cottage while the father skipped from job to job and pub to pub. He told Tehree that she must leave school and get work to help with the family income, so at sixteen she found a job as an operator in the local telephone exchange. Life at home didn't improve; there were still the beatings, the hardships and restrictions. She expected no less and she stayed at work as long as possible every day, volunteering to work overtime because work at least was safe. Then, one day when she was at home hanging out the washing, her father came from the house and grabbed her by the arm. She'd been expecting trouble because there had been an incident of the kind that inevitably roused him to utter fury. He had been laying into her younger brother for some real or imagined sin when Tehree had intervened, grown-up enough now to get between them so that the boy could run away. It was outright defiance, something which her father could neither handle nor ignore and he had brooded about it ever since.

'Get out of our lives!' he yelled at the girl. 'You're no good here, you're no good for anything! You should have been a son, not a bloody daughter. If you don't get out of our lives I swear I'll murder you all, and your mother too!'

Even though she was used to his scenes Tehree was frightened. She hadn't the slightest doubt that he was capable of murder, and if it was her presence that might drive him to it the sooner she went the better. She applied for a transfer to the Mt Gambier telephone exchange and at the age of sixteen and a half Tehree left home, convinced that without her the rest of them might lead a more normal life. Being on her own was wonderful, until the family followed her to Mt Gambier. She says it was as if her father couldn't keep away from her, even though he said he hated her so much. Her parents urged her to come and live with them. 'Why pay rent to live in the next street?' her mother asked. Tehree went back for a time but it was impossible, as bad as it had ever been and she left again, convinced that her presence only made things worse.

She went to Adelaide where she took a job with an advertising agency as a telephonist/receptionist, but she still needed more money. Her mother was perpetually short of even basic funds for housekeeping, let alone for extras such as schoolbooks and clothes for the three younger children. Besides that Tehree's own wardrobe was almost non-existent. Her father's parting contribution had been two dresses from Coles and apart from those she had no clothes suitable even for work in the office. She took an early-morning job at a riding stables, mucking out boxes and getting the horses ready for work. She showered and changed at the stables, had breakfast there and took a bus to her advertising agency. Two nights a week she went to night school to learn typing and shorthand and on Friday and Saturday nights she worked as an usherette in a cinema. The stables gave her a full day's work on Saturdays and Sundays and on Sunday nights Tehree, mindful of her mother's teachings, went to church. It was not the kind of life most seventeen-year-olds would choose.

Tehree said, 'I used to work out on a trampoline after the cinema closed at night just to help me get rid of the frustration, but at least I was getting more money and I had the horses to look forward to in the mornings.

'I had a boyfriend of sorts, a guy at the office, and he was good to me. He saw I was a country bumpkin without a clue about city life so he took me out to dinner sometimes and showed me round the town a bit. He didn't ask for anything but friendship at first but then he began to get a bit too demanding. It was perfectly natural I guess, but I wasn't ready for it and I couldn't cope. I decided the best thing was to get out of that office, right away from him.' She left the advertising agency and took a job with Mayne Nickless, a step up in the hierarchy of the business world, but before she could start work she had a letter from her mother and it immediately made the hair rise on the back of Tehree's neck. Her family had moved from Mt Gambier to Geelong by then. Her father was working with a scrap metal outfit and her mother had a job as supervisor in a catering firm.

'My mother wrote that everything was fine at home and I knew that couldn't be true, nothing had ever been fine at home. Then she said that the only thing wrong was that she was having a little trouble with a sore foot. I knew I had to go and see for myself so I went to Geelong between jobs and I'm glad I did. Mother was dragging herself off to work every day with a broken foot. She'd dropped a table on it and she was frightened of losing her job if she stayed away. I forgot about Mayne Nickless and settled back with them for a while to help her.'

She was determined to have a career of some kind, something better than the jobs she'd been doing with no clear future or particular interest for her. It was predictable that she should look for it in some branch of the Services, in an organisation with rules and rewards, uniforms, and a defined purpose. Her childhood had been an unbroken series of disorders, uncertainties, fears and disappointments, therefore uniforms and life-according-to-the-rules promised stability. Tehree applied to join the South Australian police, the Victorian police and the WRAAF.

'I'd decided that I'd go to whichever of the Services I'd applied to would take me first. It was the Air Force so I joined up with them and I loved it. I had my own room and I could sit and talk to the other girls; I was one of them, not different any more. The life was what I'd always wanted, no traumas and bashings and shouting but everything in its place and I knew I'd be good at it. I was really getting into it, I was twenty and I could see the way ahead and then suddenly everything went berserk.

'I'd finished my training and thought everything was fine when my Sergeant came and told me that my mother was ill and I'd have to go home. When I got to Geelong I found that my father had gone, walked out. He'd been supposed to pick my mother up from work the night before and she'd waited for him for hours but he didn't come. Finally she got a lift home and when she got there she found that he'd packed a couple of suitcases and disappeared. He left my mother with six cents in her purse because she'd given him what money she had the day before, and he left a stack of debts behind him. None of the bills had been paid, not rent or gas or electricity or anything, and I knew I'd have to help mother if she was going to survive. I don't think my mother had ever imagined he'd just leave her that way. You know, I can't remember a single time when I'd heard her criticise him in front of us and she'd always answer him quietly when he shouted at her. When he'd come home drunk and pass out in a chair, she'd whisper to us to go to bed before he came to. She'd had a terrible time with him but there must have been something between them still, because when he left like that she felt her life was destroyed.

'When all this happened I knew I had to make a decision. I had signed up with the Air Force for six years and that meant I couldn't be much use to my mother or the kids if I stayed in the Service. I went to see the women's Padre and talked to him for a whole day. I said, "Everything tells me I ought to get out of the Air Force and go home and I don't want to." I did get out though. There really wasn't much choice.'

After she left the Air Force Tehree took a job with American Health Studios. 'I worked with people then, people who were unhealthy and fat and lazy and I did pretty well there. I enjoyed the work and I was made State Manager, even offered a job in America but I wouldn't take it. Besides walking out on Mum it meant leaving my dogs or else putting them through all the business of travel and quarantine and I couldn't do that to them. You know, when I was little I'd thought of becoming a nun but I wasn't sure what nuns and priests really did. I guess I thought that priests helped people and nuns stayed behind stone walls and prayed for them. Either way they did it for people but I still wanted to help animals. I'd never heard of priests or nuns doing that.'

Tehree would have made a most unusual nun and I suspect that even nursing would have presented problems. She would make a super-efficient nurse for the very sick, but many of the human patients would infuriate her with their demands and complaints. Animals never demand or complain; instead they accept, and even though they have no comprehension of human care they seem to understand when someone is trying to help them. As priests and nuns serve the God of humankind Tehree works hand-in-hand with the God of animals.

She uses the word 'faith' as few of us do, without any greater embarrassment than if she were talking about a tool, a garden spade for example, but it's not faith in any God that I've ever heard of in an established church. Tehree's father was a Catholic by birth and since his eldest daughter's gender deprived him of the family right to sacrifice his firstborn to the priesthood he revenged himself by maltreating her. It should have put her off all Gods for life but somehow her mother, an Anglican, managed to substitute a God who lived close enough to touch, talk to and argue with. Tehree's God has told her to look after animals for Him, so not unreasonably she expects His help and believes she gets it. One has only to drive with her into a crowded Geelong street when she's on a mission for her animals to realise how personal the relationship is.

'I need a parking spot!' says Tehree to no-one in particular, confronted by a solid block of filled spaces. 'I need it NOW!'

Obediently one of the nearest cars backs out and lets Tehree in. 'Thanks,' she says, to her unseen helper, having expected no less. Equally, she's inclined to believe that, if she drops a brick on her toe or suffers some other minor personal disaster, it's a direct reprimand for a transgression of her own in thought, word or deed, and that it serves her right.

There were more than ten years between her father's disappearance and the beginnings of Jirrahlinga, ten years which were in some ways no easier than the earlier years had been. There was a marriage, but it was not a happy one, and Tehree is disinclined to talk freely about it.

'I married someone who'd smashed me up in a car accident,' she told me. ' We were friends and I was sorry for him and for myself. He and his family were German and when I went to live with them they all talked German whenever they were together. They looked on me as an outsider and treated me like one and it just couldn't work. In the end there was a row between us and I thought, "What am I doing here? I don't need this," and I left.'

She worked as Manager of Geelong Animal Welfare and in 1975 she was offered the job of Bellarine Shire Ranger, the first time a woman had held the position. Tehree has always had a special relationship with dogs and is a professional dog trainer. She persuaded the Queenscliff Borough and the Bellarine Shire to establish the first Dog Beach where dogs were allowed to run free, setting a precedent that has been followed in many areas round the coast. Her duties included animal rescues, stock loose on roads and a multitude of bizarre situations which can spring up out of nowhere for a Ranger, but at last she was having professional, rewarding experience with animals and with wildlife.

Her father was still missing; his absence and total silence was to last for twenty years. It should have been a period of healing for his children, a time when they could forget past nightmares and look forward, but it wasn't like that. He'd damaged them in ways they could never entirely mend and besides, they were never sure when he might come back. Tehree talked to me about the emotional legacy he'd left to her brothers and her younger sister. The elder of the two boys was constantly beaten and belittled; his father considered him a fool and a weakling and did his best to make him into both. The younger boy stood up for himself, and though he was constantly beaten and punished for doing so he may have survived better than the others. The youngest child, Tehree's sister, escaped most of the trouble because she was young enough to be protected by her mother's presence, and by the time she was a teenager he had left. Curiously, although she escaped his violence, she is still convinced it was all her fault, that it was because of her that her father left, because of her that he came back. She adored her mother and lives with an agonising sense of having somehow caused her worst moments of pain.

'What about you, Tehree?' I asked her. 'What do you feel he did to you emotionally?'

She thought for a while. 'He made me absolutely certain I was worthless. I always believed, when I was small, that I didn't really belong to my family, that they'd picked me up under a bush or adopted me or something. I was sure there was some way I was different, awful, and that all the bad things that happened were my fault.

'It's funny though, I've never been able to get over the fact that when he died I didn't have a chance to say goodbye to him. I wasn't told he was dying and I didn't get there in time. My sister was looking after him then and she told me afterwards that it was because he didn't want to see me. I don't know if that's true or not, but it makes me sad because I'd have liked to tell him that I loved him really. He had a good side, he taught me a lot. He taught me to hide my feelings and never to give in, to fight for what I believe is right. He could help others too if they needed help, he was what they call a Street Saint and a lot of people outside the family thought he was wonderful. I know it doesn't make sense but I did love him. He was my father and all I've wanted, ever since I can remember, was for him to say once, just once, that I'm not completely worthless.'

Tehree sent me a note the other day. She'd read what I'd already written about her childhood and was afraid that people might feel sorry for her. This is what she wrote.

'I don't feel I had a "poor me" childhood. I feel it was a happy childhood. Like the time when Dad dumped us at the beach and we lived in the car for six weeks, which was very traumatic for Mum, one woman alone with four children and no money, but we had a ball. It's not until you're older and have other children's experiences relayed to you that you become aware of any difference.

'The only time I remember feeling short-changed (regarding Dad) was when I made the comment that I wished he was a wharfie like Mr Gorman, the man who lived next door. Dad almost knocked me into next week, not understanding the reason I'd said it.

'Mum said, "Why on earth did you say that to your father?"

'I said it was because Mr Gorman always had time for his kids, and for us. He played games with us and so on. He knew lots of good stuff to teach us kids, cricket, beetles, rabbits, why spiders have so many legs. He was patient and understanding of little kids' questions and I believed it was because he was a wharfie.

'The truth is Mr Gorman was often on strike, that was why he had so much time. He drank like a fish and was often quite violent but I was never frightened of him.'

Tehree's fierce determination not to be 'poor me' is part of her father's legacy to her. Pride prevents what would be quite legitimate self-pity, but nothing will ever wipe out her agonising need to prove to him that she's not entirely worthless, or allow her to understand that she has already proved it.

Somehow, out of the appalling childhood and her early struggles, Tehree has emerged with Jirrahlinga. The Sanctuary doesn't exist to make money, although it couldn't continue to exist without it; nor does Tehree do her work for animals because she was trained for it or hopes to become rich through it. Jirrahlinga evolved rather as Mother Theresa's mission did in Calcutta, starting with compassion and snowballing into a functional mechanism for its application.

Compassion for animals isn't uncommon. Many people feel deeply about them; but far less usual is the will and the ability to express that compassion in practical terms. There are wonderful vets who treat wildlife free of charge, adjust their fees to the means of poverty-stricken owners and answer calls for help at any hour, at great inconvenience to themselves. Animal Liberationists do good work, but a great deal of it ends in vocalising and banner waving or, at worst, the kind of misguided lunacy that releases caged animals which have never known life in the wild, and will never survive. Tehree's work is direct, practical, and without the sentimentality that so often distorts the attitude of humans to animals.

Tehree's philosophy for Jirrahlinga is, above all, the reduction of suffering in both wild and domestic creatures and even, as in the case of her Special People, in rejected and disadvantaged human beings. She knows too that the prevention of suffering by eliminating its causes is just as important as its reduction. In the case of wildlife this can best be achieved by educating the public to know more about our wildlife and their environment. The future preservation of our native species lies, she maintains, in teaching people to know them and value them, to preserve their natural habitat and to share Australia with them in mutual respect and enjoyment of each other's company.

PART TWO

THE WILDLIFE AT JIRRAHLINGA

No single book could cover the variety of bird species, mammals, sea creatures and reptiles in the State of Victoria, nor even every one of those cared for by Tehree at Jirrahlinga. Most of the people who read this book will be familiar with all the creatures mentioned in it, but few Australians have had the opportunity to hand-raise, care for and release our wildlife, or to live with them on a day-to-day basis. For this reason this wildlife section is partly anecdotal as well as being, we hope, partly informative.

Because Tehree and I met over wildlife, because I too have been lucky enough to care for wildlife and to live with them, my animals have sometimes invaded the anecdotes. Please excuse them. They are no part of Jirrahlinga, though some of them migrated there, but they serve as examples of what to expect if you share your hearth and your heart with creatures of the wild.

Kangaroo

4 Kangaroos and Wallabies

TO THOSE OF US WHO LIVE in Australia kangaroos are commonplace, but it would have been a delight to see the disbelief on the faces of Captain Cook and his crew confronted with their first-ever kangaroo. Nobody in the Western world had ever even imagined a creature like it, and at the time of that first sighting they had no idea of how far its wonders went. It was obvious that it carried and suckled its young in a pouch on its stomach, but not that the newborn baby itself, weighing about 800 mg, a jellified, pink, hairless embryo, made a marathon journey from its mother's urogenital opening up her stomach, through her fur, to her pouch. Nor was it known that the mother is able to regulate her breeding according to the state of the season, or that a fertilised egg may remain dormant inside her, until the young she carries in her pouch leaves it at the age of nine months.

The kangaroo and the wallaby have always been the subject of misconceptions. For a long time, in the days when Australia was a lowly colonial backwater, foreigners believed that the streets of our cities swarmed with wild kangaroos, obstructing both pedestrians and traffic. Today it is the opposite: there's a belief, widely held among Animal Liberationists overseas, that the kangaroo is an endangered species, callously slaughtered by red-neck Aussie farmers. In fact the kangaroo population is on the rise, largely because farmers have greatly improved its food supply by clearing land for grazing and by creating dams and other water points. The kangaroo never had it so good, and since its natural increase is in direct proportion to the availability of nourishment it was never in less danger than it is today.

It's true that kangaroos do get shot and some of them, a very small proportion of the total, are killed by the 'If It Moves Shoot It' heroes who find pleasure in killing for killing's sake. By far the greater number are culled under license, firstly because they are grazing animals and large herds pose unacceptable competition to stock for the available pasture, particularly in drought conditions. Secondly they may be culled in an area where their natural increase results in such overcrowding that they themselves may run out of food and starve. It's true also that the meat and skins of the culled animals can be sold commercially, but to date there is no wholesale slaughter of kangaroos for profit. In Victoria at least they are protected, and unauthorised shooting is illegal.

Serious kangaroo farming may well develop in the future, for their meat is low in fat and high in protein, and given the right conditions they breed almost as freely as the proverbial rabbit. Having said that I confess that I have never eaten kangaroo meat, because I have raised a great many of them and it would seem too close to cannibalism. I love and respect the kangaroo, its character, its beauty and its lifestyle in its proper environment, the Australian countryside. As foster-children in a human family or in a Shelter they are only on loan, however closely they may bond with you. The time will come, as it does with all wild things, when they crave freedom with their own kind, and the greatest gift you can give your charges is to equip them for that freedom.

The genus *Macropus* – a solemn Greek-based word which simply means 'long-foot' – includes a variety of wallabies, kangaroos and wallaroos, but the Eastern Grey kangaroo is by far its best known representative in Victoria, and indeed in the whole eastern section of Australia. The Red kangaroo is the dominant species in Central and Western Australia, the Western Grey inhabits the south-west of the continent and the Antalipine wallaroo is confined to the far North. Wallabies of various kinds can be found in many parts of Tasmania and the mainland, distributed according to their preference of habitat.

Wallabies are diverse and fascinating animals but on the eastern Australian mainland the Eastern Grey kangaroo is our constant companion, a familiar presence. Leave the outer suburbs of Melbourne and drive for a few minutes into any area of moderate size farms, into cropping or grazing country still containing the odd patch of scrub or trees, and the Eastern Grey kangaroo will be there. Look for him at dusk or early in the morning for in the daytime he'll be sleeping, somewhere in the shade.

Kangaroos

Most of Jirrahlinga's kangaroos, and indeed all those that arrive in Wildlife Shelters, are very young, often the victims of road accidents where the mother has been killed and the neonate or juvenile rescued. Rescue and treatment of an injured adult is seldom advisable; their fear of humans means that they undergo terrible stress and often damage themselves further by resisting help; euthanasia is far more merciful than pain and terror combined. Baby kangaroos and wallabies, however, take the transfer to human care in their stride, until they reach the age when all their instincts urge them to be among their own kind. Then you face an identity problem, unless they have been raised with other young kangaroos.

Jirrahlinga, of course, always has plenty of young marsupials, but one of the drawbacks in small Wildlife Shelters is that they are not always able to raise their animals with a mate of its own age and species. Ideally you would pair off a baby Eastern Grey male with a

This joey would be about a year old, but still returns to the pouch for security and a feed.

young female, a female wombat baby with a male and so on. In that way, when the time comes for them to be released they are not released on their own and they have some idea of what they really are. A singleton of any kind bonds too strongly with the human who feeds it, and separation from that particular human causes immense stress. On both sides, I might add, because releasing such an animal to an unknown future will seem as bad to you as abandoning your only child to a foreign boarding school from which there are no holidays.

It was because of a young male Eastern Grey that I first met Tehree, a year or so after the Ash Wednesday fires. He was a good example of the problems inherent in rearing a singleton and inevitably bonding too closely with the animal. He had driven down to Jirrahlinga from Kilmore in the car with me, his habitual exuberance under restraint because he was in a chaff bag, tied tastefully round his neck with twine. He had an enquiring disposition and if free would probably have chosen to make the journey on my lap, holding on to the steering wheel to get a clear view of the road. As he'd been with me for nearly a year and was a well-grown adolescent this was undesirable if we were to arrive in one piece. Like all young kangaroos he was a creature of charm and intelligence, his only drawback being that as yet he had no idea that he was a kangaroo and not a human.

Tehree took me to a small wooden gate leading into an enclosure of young kangaroos. They were feeding, playing together or standing with their tummies stuck out and grooming themselves luxuriously, as happy a band of young marsupial thugs as you'd hope to see. We untied the twine round my 'roo's neck, extracted him from the chaff-bag and directed his attention to his natural peer group. He stiffened, his ears shot forward, his film-star lashed eyes grew huge and he clutched my hand with one of his own, utterly confounded by the strange creatures in front of him. Just so must stone-age Aborigines have viewed their first white man, with incredulity, fear and no conception that they too might belong to the same race. We stayed frozen together for almost an hour. I squatted beside him while he leaned heavily against me, staring at the other 'roos until Tehree said, 'This is no good, we'll have to put him in with them. We pushed the young 'roo, trembling, through the gate where he

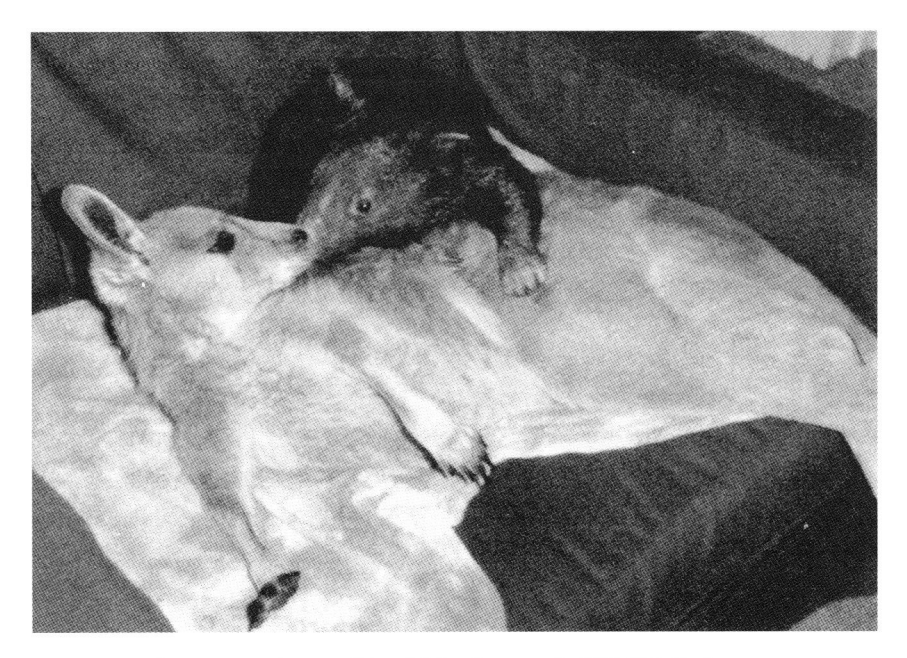

Some very strange friendships happen in Wildlife Refuges. This particular wombat/kangaroo friendship developed at Willowmavin, the author's Refuge at Kilmore.

promptly turned his back on the others and gazed imploringly at me through the bars. I realised that all this was old-hat to Tehree, knew that he'd be fine in a day or two and felt ashamed that it was so hard for me to walk away. We went back to the enclosure before I left, peering round a corner so that my abandoned child shouldn't see us. He was still standing at the gate, gazing sadly in the direction he'd last seen me, and I gulped.

'He'll be alright,' said Tehree briskly. 'Give me a ring in about three days and I'll let you know how he's doing. We'll look after him.'

I rang her after two days, unable to get him out of my mind and feeling like the worst kind of traitor. He was still watching from the gate, she said, and I felt even worse, but Tehree seemed unworried. Sure enough, on the third day he simply turned away from the gate and became a kangaroo. This period of three days seems to have some special significance with wildlife. Orphans which arrive shocked, bereft and uncooperative to the point of refusing food and comfort will resist all help for three days, then suddenly settle into your arms, grab the feeding bottle in both paws and accept you as their foster mother. So it was that after three days of limbo-existence my little 'roo joined the mob, and when they were released into a suitable, supervised area he went with them, hopefully to eventual fatherhood and fulfilment as a dominant male kangaroo. Later Tehree told me that on his first night she'd slept in the straw of the kangaroo shed with him, so that he wouldn't be lonely.

The adolescent male kangaroo is particularly explicit in letting you know when, mentally and physically, he's ready for more appropriate company. We all know about pubescent human boys; they are sexually inquisitive, not to mention dirty-minded, and kangaroos at that stage are much the same. On more than one occasion an adolescent male has embarrassed me by seizing one of my visiting lady friends round the waist from behind, producing an admirable erection and hammering it into her legs in an instinctive quest for sex. This is less of a success with some women than with others, and one should try to explain that it is actually an innocent form of kangaroo compliment, while making a mental note that the young gentleman would be better off among other kangaroos.

Adult male kangaroos are substantially bigger than females and should be treated with considerable respect. A male Eastern Grey can weigh up to 66 kg and stand nearly two metres high, with arm and chest muscles that would intimidate a heavyweight boxer. Indeed, he can box quite efficiently with his arms but his immensely powerful hind legs with their armour-plated toes are his real weapon. With his weight balanced on his tail and his opponent held to his chest the hind legs can sweep upwards, the sharp, horned toes tearing open the victim's front like twin knives. Two kangaroo males, challenging each other at mating time and using the same tactics, look very much like two boxers in the ring. Since they both fight the same way they know better than to be held, but there are cases of humans being killed by kangaroos that hold them and rip them apart. If you get close to a large male, take note that when he stands up and makes a sound like a deep cough you should retreat, discreetly, humbly and at some speed. Beware, if you meet him, the male Red kangaroo who is even larger than the Eastern Grey. He can weigh up to 85 kg, and his nature is generally more aggressive.

Although the Red kangaroo isn't a native of Victoria individuals occasionally turn up in Wildlife Shelters, usually as babies, having been picked up by someone coming down from the inland. Occasionally that someone is misguided enough to think they can keep the animal at home and the Red kangaroo, being a tough customer, may survive some very unconventional rearing methods, but is not recommended as a domestic pet once he's grown. Tehree had just such a young Red kangaroo passed on to her at Jirrahlinga, and asked the woman who brought him what his diet had been.

'Twisties,' she was told, 'and dog food but he gets ice-cream and a glass of wine at night. Of course he sleeps on our bed.' Tehree set about weaning the animal onto a more suitable life-style and diet, keeping it with other kangaroos and taking it a glass of wine in the evening, but gradually reducing the wine and adding water until it became a teetotaller. The shock of going cold turkey at the same time as it was released into the bush would have been too traumatic.

I too have found that kangaroos are inclined to alcoholism. Rachel, a particularly nubile Eastern Grey, was hooked on gin and tonic. She was soft-furred and delectably rounded, with eyes like Audrey Hepburn and she was intensely sociable. We had asked some friends round for a midday drink and Rachel, joining us unnoticed, sampled a glass of gin and tonic standing on a low coffee table. When the glass's owner turned to get his drink she had it in both hands and was lapping up the contents with great relish. Thereafter she made her presence felt whenever we had visitors, pestering them for a sip or more of their gin. It never seemed to have much effect on her and luckily no other form of alcohol appealed to her; gin and tonic remained Rachel's tipple and we were careful to keep it out of her reach. The habit of drinking out of a human drinking vessel, obviously connected in her mind with delicious gin, became fixed. She preferred her formula out of a mug rather than a bottle and would lap from it standing like a child, mug in two hands and tummy stuck out, but one had to watch in case she dropped the mug on the brick floor when she'd finished.

Rachel came to a tragic end: she was bitten by a snake one day in the kangaroo enclosure, jumped backwards and in doing so broke her back. We didn't know about the back at first. She was given antivenene and the snakebite symptoms disappeared, but she was paralysed and x-rays showed that her spine was in two pieces. There was no alternative but to put her down. This is not an uncommon accident for a young kangaroo; they are designed for forward movement and only jump backwards involuntarily when frightened Their tail is a continuation of their spinal column and an unwary backward jump can exert too much pressure on the vertebrae.

In the wild state the young kangaroo must learn everything from its mother, how to interact with other kangaroos, how and what to eat, what constitutes danger and a host of other things. Such knowledge could be simply the result of genetic instinct plus parental guidance, but young Eastern Greys also display a capacity to learn from humans that can only be attributed to intelligence. Once they are leaving their pouch and living in a partly human environment, they learn very rapidly, what is allowed and what is forbidden. Although kangaroos are herd animals, their behaviour conditioned by herd behaviour, they are capable of individual intelligence and they have a memory. We raised a young Red kangaroo, an involuntary immigrant from the north, whom we named Qantas. He became a strapping young fellow with ideas of his own and I was on the point of approaching the Conservation Department to arrange his release when he solved the problem himself.

The back paddocks of Willowmavin Stud were divided by a creek beyond which was a hillside of thick scrub and trees, and in the evenings a large mob of Eastern Greys came out to the creek flats to graze. I walked down there one evening with Qantas at my heels and unlike most of his hand-raised Eastern Grey cousins, who are afraid of their own kind at first, Qantas took an immediate interest. His ears went up, he rose to his full height, then bounded towards them at full speed. They saw me, saw him coming and set off back into the bush with Qantas lost in the mob. There was nothing I could do about it and anyway he was old enough to be released. We never saw him again and I worried about him, feeling guilty because of his unorthodox departure. About six years later a neighbour came to visit me.

'A most extraordinary thing happened the other evening,' she said. 'I've had an English couple staying with me and they wanted to see kangaroos. I drove them down that dirt road along the creek, only a couple of miles away and there was a big mob of Greys grazing in a paddock. I got out of the car and walked over to the fence and there was a huge Red buck among them. I didn't think there were any Reds down here. He stood up and looked at me and then rushed towards me. He jumped right over the fence. I ran back to the car and this 'roo stood there a few yards away, just staring at me. D'you think he might be dangerous?'

I said, 'No, not dangerous, that was Qantas.' Half of me was happy and half was jealous because if it had been me that he came to I'd have learned so much more about kangaroo memory. I'd love to know what he'd have done if I'd called him by name, but at least I knew that he was well and he'd survived. I drove down that road on many evenings looking for Qantas, walked down through the paddocks and called him, but the mob was never there and he never came. The interesting thing was that he'd remembered human contact well enough to come back to the woman on the road, without fear or aggression.

There must be many cases of baby marsupials, Reds, Eastern Greys, wallabies and wombats picked up and taken home by people whose intentions are entirely good, but whose competence to care for wildlife is non-existent. Instead of seeking expert help at the start they embark on a downward spiral of mistakes and often quite unconscious cruelty to the animal. At worst they lose interest in the creature, find it a nuisance and commit the ultimate cruelty of indifference and neglect. Tehree tells of a female joey that came her way when she was Shire Ranger. This little kangaroo was a good example of the truly appalling things that can happen to a young marsupial when it falls into the wrong hands.

'I got a call one day from someone who was worried about the children next door who had a pet kangaroo. They'd even been seen swinging it round by the tail and now it had just disappeared. I went round and asked the children's mother about it. She said someone had given it to her kids as a pet, but lately it had some marks on it and didn't seem too well so she'd put it in the chook yard.

'When I went there it was dreadful, the joey was totally stressed, clinging to a piece of rope hanging from the mesh roof. The place stank, it was covered with filth and there was no shelter of any kind. The little 'roo was in a terminal state of shock, stiff from head to foot and she didn't seem to know I was there. She was covered with sores, she had mange and later we found that her tail was broken. I rang the Department of Natural Resources and Environment and said I was confiscating her under a charge of cruelty, then took her round to the vet. He had to give her muscle relaxants and treat her for stress before we could do anything else, but she was in such bad shape we decided we'd better put her down.

'I thought I'd give her a bottle of milk before that happened and as she took the milk the look of absolute trust and relief she gave us made both the vet and me think again; we thought she should have a chance to live. We got permission to keep her at the Sanctuary and it was a long haul to get her right again, but worth every moment of it. We called her Splinter and she was such a tame, affectionate animal that we used her a lot in entertaining people from overseas. In fact she was doing just that at an RSL function when the Duke of Kent, who was visiting Australia then, had to be reminded that it was time to leave because he was so enchanted by her.

'She lived with the other adult kangaroos at Jirrahlinga and she must have got together with one of the males. We didn't know about this until one day she came to me, scratching at my side and then moving away, so I followed her. I'd no idea she was pregnant, I thought she just wanted company or a cuddle, but to my amazement she took up the birthing position, sitting with her tail underneath her, sticking out between her legs. About fifteen minutes later I actually saw the birth of a kangaroo and not many people have had that privilege.'

One of Jirrahlinga's permanent residents, a female Eastern Grey kangaroo named Skippy, had her twenty-third birthday party the other day and this is a great age for a kangaroo. Skippy is part of the Sanctuary's furniture, fond of food, permanently at large and usually resting in what can only be described as a 'somnolent posture' on the grass, as comfortable an old lady as you could wish to see.

The Duke of Kent and Splinter got on so well he had to be reminded it was time to leave.

Skippy spent her early life in a children's camp. There's a photo of her playing with a child, now a man in his late twenties, which establishes her age. When she was an early teenager the camp's management changed and a compulsively hygienic new administration decided that kangaroo droppings and children shouldn't mix. In my opinion the new management must have been totally ignorant of what children get up to in camps, but be that as it may it was decreed that Skippy must go. A concerned wildlife carer, who knew she was unsuitable for release and who didn't want her to be put down, rang Jirrahlinga.

Teenage kangaroos are thought to be approaching the end of their allotted span and Jirrahlinga agreed to take her in for the short time left to her. Instead they now harbour what, in kangaroo terms, should be a doddering geriatric but is actually an active matriarch, in possession of all her faculties. Tehree admits that she's puzzled by Skippy's prolonged survival.

'She's fed normal, healthy kangaroo food,' she said, 'but as she's got older we've given her a warm bed at night. Maybe it's the spoiling she gets – from the staff, not me – because she knows only too well where the Kiosk is and she has a passion for Anzac biscuits. We let her have a young joey who'd been born here to roam with her for company and to learn good manners from her. He learned where the Anzac biscuits came from quick enough and she didn't like it, so she turned on him and sent him packing. She gives enormous pleasure to people who come to the Sanctuary though, especially disabled people because she has no fear at all of wheelchairs. We hope she'll be with us for a long time to come.'

Wallabies

Of all the wallabies distributed throughout Australia, Rock wallabies, Hare wallabies, Nailtail wallabies and many more, Victoria is home only to the Swamp wallaby and the Red-neck wallaby. The latter is found from southern Queensland, eastern NSW and southern Victoria to Tasmania where it is known as the Bennetts wallaby and its population reaches pest proportions. The Red-neck is large as wallabies go, and this is probably the secret of its success, since the smaller varieties such as the Hare Wallaby have suffered badly from our introduced predators, the fox and the cat. Some of the smaller species are extinct, others in danger of extinction. A healthy adult Swamp wallaby, like the Red-neck, is big enough to look after itself, and the juveniles of both these larger species are at risk from predators only if they stray too far from their mother's pouch.

Although wallabies belong to the family Macropodidae each wallaby species is a specialised entity, and they all differ from kangaroos and from other macropods in size, preferred habitat, behaviour and a dozen biological features. Jirrahlinga gets both the Victorian species brought in for care, the majority of them Swamp wallabies from the Otway area. Alongside the kangaroos they look squat, placid and less than athletic, but according to Tehree this is far from the truth.

'They're far flightier than a kangaroo,' she says. 'They'll panic if they're chased and simply lose their heads, bash themselves about and get hurt. On the other hand baby wallabies are far easier to raise

Swamp wallaby and joey.

than kangaroo joeys. They're tougher in a lot of ways, and when they're out of the pouch they're very inquisitive and agile. I've seen a young wallaby, quite a small one, hop from the floor onto a sofa, off the seat onto the sofa's back and then up onto a shelf just to see what's there. A young kangaroo would never do that, it couldn't. When young wallabies reach a certain stage they suddenly cease to want to know you, however closely they've bonded. They suddenly transform from loving children, dependent on their carer, to wild creatures, and it's a mystery how it happens. They just don't need you any more!'

Raising baby kangaroos and wallabies

In case your car hits a marsupial mother some dark night on a country road, and you find yourself alone in charge of her baby, here are Tehree's notes on its care and raising.

Do's and Don'ts as advised by Tehree

'You may never have thought about raising a baby kangaroo or wombat but don't think it can't happen to you, because if you ever drive on country roads it may. If you should find a dead female on the roadside, look round for a baby nearby and check the female's pouch, in case there's a joey there. If it's a 'pinkie', still unhaired, you must take it off the teat very slowly and gently, or if necessary cut the teat from the dead mother. Wrap the joey up firmly in a cloth or towel, because the mother's pouch is very firm and expands as the joey grows. Keep the baby warm but don't overheat it, and take it to the nearest Wildlife Shelter or the Zoo. The police will direct you to the nearest Shelter and they, or the Zoo, will be able to give you advice on feeding and raising it. The Shelter will take it if you can't or don't want to care for it yourself, but if you're game to take it home and raise it, these are the rules.

'First of all, if you're going to take on the raising of a little marsupial you should realise that it's going to take up a lot of your time. Furthermore, if you're feeding it round the clock you're going to get very tired, so don't start unless you think you'll do the job to the end; it's not fair to the joey. Remember too that from the beginning the joey's going to need plenty of body contact, cuddling if you like. In the mother's pouch they can feel her heart beat and every movement she makes. Suddenly taking that closeness out of their life causes them dreadful stress, so you must be a substitute mother.

'Don't on any account take it home and feed it cow's milk. Use a low lactose formula Digestelac which can be bought from chemists, or Divetelac or Wombaroo which you can get from Veterinary clinics, because marsupial milk has a much higher protein and lower fat content than cow's milk. Also you'll need a special marsupial teat. If you can't get a marsupial teat a 20 ml syringe with a short length of plastic intravenous tubing pushed onto the spout is quite effective. The soft, pliable plastic tubing can be pushed into the joey's mouth and even if it doesn't want to suck you can get some food down its throat. Don't worry about Pentavite which supplies Vitamin B, they don't need it.

'Joeys need to be fed little and often, every two hours if they're unfurred and every three to four hours if their fur has grown. This means all through the night as well, right around the clock. The best way, when you've got used to your joey and understand it when it calls for food, is to feed it on demand. Don't get too fussed if it doesn't want to eat for the first two or three days after you get it, just keep on trying to get a little into it at a time and it'll come round. At Jirrahlinga we often allow baby wombats to lie on their backs to feed, because that's how they do it in the pouch. The Shelter person you take the joey to in the beginning will show you an artificial pouch and tell you how to make one; if you're lucky they may lend or give you one. They're easy to make and you'll need enough to wash them when they're dirty. Small joeys are like premature babies and they need to be kept at a pouch temperature of about 35 to 38 degrees, human body temperature. If they're unfurred they'll need a moisturiser on their skin because the mother's pouch is warm and moist, and you don't want their skin to dry out. Baby marsupials need to be kept reasonably quiet too, so don't let the kids keep poking it and pulling it out of its pouch, or go showing it to people yourself.

'After feeding you should gently wipe its anus, along the bottom of its tail, with some oiled cotton wool, so that it's stimulated to urinate and defecate. Its mother cleans it up the same way, for the same purpose. As it gets older give it a regular toilet spot lined with newspaper. You'll find joeys are very easy to toilet-train. Leave a rock on the newspaper and when you start leave one or two of the joey's scats, the dried faeces, on the paper so that he can get his own scent. At Jirrahlinga they have access to the scats of other 'roos because eating adult droppings can help the young ones develop their own stomach flora.

'If you have cats, don't let a young joey play where the cats have toiletted. Cats carry toxaplamosis, and it's deadly.

'The regular bottle-feeding stage lasts until the joey is about nine months old when it starts to leave the pouch for short periods, and weaning begins. You may be surprised when the joey scratches under the grass and nibbles the earth, but the earth appears to have some effect on the joey's faeces which gradually change from soft yellow into the firm pellets of the adult as it learns to eat solid food. Bottle feeds are still necessary but at longer intervals, because the joey in the wild suckles from his mother's teat until it's eighteen months old. In the bush, by this time, she might well have another pouch baby on one of her four teats, but the older joey will always suckle from the teat it used from birth.

'Remember that in the wild, until it is completely weaned, it has access to its mother's pouch all the time. It's the one certain shelter in the joey's life and the pouch you give it will be the same. Let it get in and out of its pouch as it wants to between feeds, but keep the pouch where it can see it, because that's its security. It'll gradually get more adventurous and stay out for longer, but even if you leave it outside on the grass it should be in an enclosure where nothing can get at it, and the pouch should be close by, where it can get into it. Joeys should have access to grass at all times when they're being weaned, and to grated or chopped carrot, broccoli or silver beet and occasionally apple. They should also be able to get at soil, so have a play pen and a digging place otherwise your garden will suffer.

'Finally, accept the fact that one day it will have to be released. Before that it must learn that it's a 'roo, meet others of its own kind and forget about people. The best way is to pass it on to a Wildlife Shelter where it can mix with others and learn from them.

'Don't ever be too proud to take advice from the experts. Raising baby animals is a learning curve; we all make mistakes and learn from them so take advantage of the people who've done it before. If you're worried about your foster child ring an established wildlife carer or the Zoo and follow their advice. On no account think, "I'll just try this or that" because young wildlife are fragile. There are rules you've got to abide by if your time and trouble and love are to have a happy ending.

Feeding a young Red kangaroo

5   Wombats

ALTHOUGH IT ISN'T in recognised wombat country, Jirrahlinga gets a steady supply of orphaned and adult wombats from other parts of the State. Wombats are regarded as vermin in the part of Victoria which lies east of the Melbourne/Sydney railway line, where they occur in large numbers, digging unwelcome burrows and damaging fences. West of the railway wombats are quite scarce and are protected, so depending on your location you may or may not be lucky/unlucky enough to get an intake of wombats. Not everyone in the world is a born wombat lover or, indeed, vice versa, but they are unique animals and raising them is an experience that no wildlife carer should miss.

Many of my early meetings with Tehree involved adolescent wombats, candidates for halfway housing at Jirrahlinga, and most of them came to me from the Kinglake area, orphaned by road accidents. The country to the east of Kilmore and across the railway line is exactly the kind of hilly, forested country that wombats love. The earth is soft, moist and diggable, hollow logs are everywhere and apart from the risk of crossing roads life is altogether wombat-friendly. It seemed that the Kinglake wombats failed to take the roads seriously because we almost always had one or more in residence, anywhere between semi-haired infancy and adulthood. Most of them came as babies because while a wombat mother may be killed by a car the baby in her pouch, protected by her body, is often unharmed.

Although wombats can move alarmingly fast their method of crossing roads is often disastrously slow; indifferent eyesight and a total absence of car-awareness mean that they cross at their leisure, stopping suicidally to stare into approaching headlights. Wombats have few predators once they are grown, and I suspect that they believe themselves to be stronger and heavier than any motor car. Certainly the danger to the driver who hits a full-grown wombat is almost as great as to the victim, which can be large and amazingly solid, and many cars have rolled or spun off the road and been wrecked in such collisions. Wombats are said to be the heaviest ani-

Mini (top wombat) menaces a male. (See page 62)

mal, size-for-weight, in the world and if you pick up even a small, football-size baby you will wonder whether it has a lead lining under its skin.

In spite of its weight there are few things more calculated to arouse the human maternal instinct than a baby wombat burrowing into your arms, its lips making sucking motions, its tiny paws kneading your fingers. When it starts to leave the pouch it will follow you nose-to-heel as it would have followed its natural mother, climb into your lap at every opportunity and fall heavily asleep there, and in its waking moments play captivating, childlike games. The latter become less captivating and more destructive as it gets older but by that time it should be housed in a secure outdoor wombat enclosure to preserve your furniture, your skirting boards and your sanity. Before we built a totally wombat-proof enclosure at Willowmavin Stud the house acquired deckled edges like old-fashioned note-paper because the young wombats resented their exclusion from an environment they considered their own, and tried to chew their way back inside. House interiors have even greater appeal for young wombats than the exteriors, being furnished and trimmed with nice, tender wood on which they can practice with their chisel-sharp front teeth and finger length claws, in preparation for later life.

Wombats are naturally solitary animals and each one is an individual, far more so than the kangaroo which, being a herd animal, is subject to the behavioural laws of its species. The wombat also has one of the flattest, least expressive faces in the animal kingdom, thereby making it difficult to judge its mood or its mood changes. Dogs, cats, horses and indeed most other animals find it quite easy to convey their feelings to humans; laid-back ears, bared teeth, hostile noises or arched backs all send an unmistakable message. A wombat communicates only by tone of voice and a limited body language, both of which can be deceptive and the results of misinterpretation explosive.

Tehree, who of course has had more than her share of wombats, once had a particular pet wombat named Bimbi. He had been raised by a family who let him go to school regularly with their children and to the supermarket on Saturday mornings besides other non-wombat activities, and he was consequently too humanised to be suitable for release into the wild. On the other hand he got on well with dogs, cats and children and was generally regarded as a social asset, but being a wombat he had a strong personality and his own standards for the behaviour of humans.

Tehree and Hamish had some friends staying with them and they were painting the house, Bob and another guest helping paint while Bob's children and Bimbi were playing in the garden. Bob started a friendly hassle with Tehree about something and she said, 'If you don't shut up I'll sool the wombat onto you!'

'What, that fat little thing?' said Bob with scorn, 'Don't make me laugh!'

Bimbi detached himself from his game and lumbered over towards Bob making the typical wombat noise, something between heavy breathing and a hiss, which can mean anything from peace to all-out war. Still amused, Bob bent down and made his own version of wom-

'Tehree ... once had a particular pet wombat named Bimbi' (page 60)

bat noises back, presumably the wrong noises because they had a disastrous effect and Bimbi charged. One moment he was a fat, hairy little toy and the next he was solid bone and muscle, hell-bent on destruction. It's said that wombats have been clocked at 40 kph, which is roughly the speed at which Bimbi chased Bob round the garden. There was a seat alongside a garden table and when Bob leapt onto it Bimbi leapt onto it too.

According to Tehree, who by this time was helpless with laughter, Bob's next move was to grab the branch of a tree above his head and to try to pull his legs up under his chin while Bimbi menaced his ankles from below.

'For God's sake stop laughing and get this brute away from me!' roared Bob, genuinely frightened. 'Tell him I didn't mean it!'

Wombats are naturally dominant animals and in my opinion the female can be deadlier than the male, once she's mature. I've seen females give larger males a terrible roughing up which the male made no attempt to return. We had a female wombat named Mini who was with us for nearly two years. For the first nine months she was a delight but thereafter she became unpredictable, still enchanting on her good days but lethal on others, or when crossed. Not only did she terrorise visiting male wombats but two successive horse vets, who tried to help me drench her, were forced to clear the metre high enclosure fence in one bound. The second vet, who was six foot eight inches tall, turned when he'd made his leap and glared at the triumphant Mini, still making heavy-breathing threats on the other side.

'She always was a bitch!' he said, heading without dignity for his car. 'She can go without a drench.'

Mini's most spectacular performance was on the night when we gave a party for about twenty of Kilmore's senior citizens. We couldn't seat twenty people so we'd planned a buffet meal, borrowed a trestle table from the race club, covered it with a cloth and loaded it with food. I was nervous about the party because some of the guests didn't know each other, while others didn't get on well with those they did know. When they arrived I saw things would indeed be sticky. They entered the house with an air of suspicion, reluctantly accepted a drink and stood well apart from each other, as if they were waiting for some signal to bring them to life.

Mini was having a particularly good day; we'd been for a walk, we'd had a game and in my desperation it came to me that the sight of such a well-socialised little wombat might prove a catalyst for our guests. Something clearly had to be done to save the party so I slipped outside and invited Mini in. Once inside the living room Mini took stock of the guests, understood the problem immediately and proceeded to liven things up. She set off round the perimeter of the room like a Formula 1 Ferrari while the Kilmore elders dodged and spilled their drinks on each other, squealing in alarm. On the second circuit she passed the buffet table, seized the corner of the tablecloth in her teeth as she went, and kept going at full throttle.

There are people who claim to be able to pull a tablecloth out from under a setting and leave the setting intact on the table but this was not a skill Mini possessed. On the other hand she had got the party going brilliantly. By the time everyone had helped to clean up the mess, declaring that they didn't mind at all eating food that had been on the floor and become as mixed-up as a chop suey, they were all friends. Mini, breathless but delighted with her success, got into an armchair, registered innocence and enjoyed the compliments heaped on her by the guests.

'Isn't she a sweet little thing?' said an octogenarian, leaning heavily on a walking stick. 'Do you think you could get me one just like her, dear? I lost my old pussy cat last month.' I looked at Mini, in whose mouth butter would have remained unmelted, thought grimly of her darker moments, and I swear she winked.

When Mini was rising two she was released. A young male wombat about her own age had arrived a few months earlier and to everyone's surprise Mini accepted him. He could even move about her enclosure without her charging him or slashing at him with her teeth. We kept them in together, handling them only when strictly necessary, giving them hollow logs to sleep in and feeding them on their natural food. They were released together one moonlit night under the supervision of a Conservation Department Ranger, in forested hills thick with fallen logs and where the ground was soft and easy for digging. Because they had formed a relationship they were better off than most released wombats, and may well have mated.

The Common wombat is very reluctant to breed in captivity, and though every Zoo, Wildlife Park and Shelter in the country has its quota of wombats, male and female, there have been only three cases of a successful captive mating until this spring. Now Jirrahlinga has produced a fourth baby and Tehree, in company with her entire staff, is justifiably proud.

'Wombats really are loners,' she says, 'and they very rarely co-habit, but the male and the female that produced our little one have lived together for years. They have a really close, affectionate relationship and this year, after they mated, they still stayed together which is even more surprising. We didn't know they'd mated but to our great delight we saw a movement in the female's pouch and found she had a baby inside it.

'It was hard to wait until we could see it properly but I was sitting quietly near their pen one day, hoping to get a photo, when the baby left the pouch and started slowly to crawl round her mother's tummy. The male was lying beside her and he just sniffed at the baby and made small, snuffling sounds, then went back to sleep. There was no sign of aggression, and male wombats aren't noted for paternal tolerance. The baby walked over the mother's side and went back into the pouch.

'It was a wonderful thing to watch it – first a tiny paw and then the nose coming out of the pouch – but then the whole relationship between the two wombats is very exciting, and the birth in captivity is very rare.'

One of the saddest wombat fates is that of the babies picked up by well meaning citizens and raised in an urban environment, which either escape or are abandoned when their erstwhile benefactors tire of them. Tehree was called to Melbourne one night to capture and remove a wombat who had been wrecking gardens in Richmond, close to the Channel 9 Studios. She and Hamish, who is not among the world's great wombat lovers, drove to town equipped with a catching net and sack, arrived at the address given and found the family sitting on the lawn. They were shown newly dug holes, identified wombat scats in the garden and set about tracking the culprit down. The two neighbouring gardens also bore evidence of wombat

The parents met at Jirrahlinga, and (unusually for wombats in captivity) mated. Their offspring was only the fourth to be born in captivity.

A WOMBAT BORN IN CAPTIVITY

The baby wombat peers out of the backward-facing pouch, and puts out a tentative pink paw.

presence and Tehree ventured further, into the grounds of Channel 9 where the night watchman told her that he'd indeed seen a large, strange animal hanging round at night.

'I thought it might be some kind of big cat,' he said, 'but it made a funny sort of noise, like this.' He breathed heavily and clicked his teeth.

'That was a wombat,' said Tehree.

She and Hamish blocked off access to Channel 9 and the garden next to it, switched on the lights in the garden of the second house and were pleased to find the wombat lying quite peacefully on the lawn. The butterfly net and sack were brought into play, the wombat secured and taken back to Jirrahlinga. It was a good example of a badly brought up wombat, humanised to the point where it was found to be incapable of normal wombat life, a young female who had come to believe that food came only in bowls and refused to touch anything growing out of the ground. Tehree had gradually to lower her feeding bowl into the earth, covering the food with soil until, smelling it, she was forced to dig for it and acquire natural tastes. A wombat pen and a hollow log filled with straw baffled her; she considered it simply unfit to sleep in, but given a pillow and a blanket she rolled herself into a blanket cocoon, crawled inside the pillow case and slept. It was three months before she learned to dig properly, eat wombat food and drink water that had not been mixed with milk.

Another heavily urbanised wombat that Tehree rescued in the city was wearing a dog collar bearing the name 'Poochie' and had similar identity problems.

There are many cases to prove that wombats have a long memory and lasting affections, and I learned this myself through Evans, a wombat of great character and charm. He also proved, for some time at least, that release can be successful, and his eventual death had nothing to do with his early years in the company of humans.

Growing up he was a splendid house-wombat. All the other animals liked him and he was gentle with them, even allowing Maud the magpie to sit on his back and pull his neck hair, and sleeping heavily in our armchairs together with the Jack Russells or baby kangaroos. He came for long walks with me and developed a talent for finding mushrooms in the mushroom season, running in front of me and stopping to show me when he found one, exactly as a truffle-pig points out truffles to its owner in France. He became so much at home round the place that when he began to wander off for a matter of days we didn't worry. Our property ran down to a gully and a creek, there was a wild, scrubby hillside beyond that and wombats were not uncommon in the area. If Evans had found suitable habitat and company close to home it seemed logical to accept his choice. After he had been gone for a matter of months we congratulated ourselves on a successful and painless return to the wild.

Our house at Willowmavin Stud had ceiling-to-floor sliding windows opening onto an area of grass and fruit trees, and I always left my bedroom window open four or five inches when I went to bed. At about 3 o'clock one morning, months after he'd left us, there was a crash as the window was driven back into its socket, a burst of heavy-breathing and a cold nose pushed violently over the side of my bed into my face. I turned on the light and saw that Evans had matured into a monster wombat, shiny of coat, bright of eye and excited far beyond the bounds of restraint at being home. He was so delighted with himself that he was uncontrollable, jumping at me, rolling to have his tummy rubbed, scuttling round the room and bumping into things like a huge puppy. I called him through the house to the kitchen and fed him raisin bread, which he'd always loved, to calm him. When we went back to the bedroom he was manageable. He gave me a gentle nudge, walked out through the open window into the darkness and vanished.

He came back several times at three or four month intervals, and once after a break of nine months. Every time he seemed bigger, heavier and more exuberant. At the end of an hour or so he would simply take his leave but each time he was harder to control, charging my bed when he came in so that it slid clean across the room. I'd kneel in the middle of it saying, 'Evans, stop it! Stop it!' and if a wombat can laugh, he was laughing. I kept a pair of gumboots permanently beside my bed, pulling them on when he arrived because in his excitement he'd chop at my shins, meaning no harm but inflicting severe damage, for the love-nips of childhood now removed sizeable chunks of flesh. I looked forward to his visits, dreaded them and yet hoped they would never stop, knowing that if they did I'd worry about him.

Evans met his end by tragic chance one foggy, evil night, the same night that our younger son also died. We learned of Evan's death first, setting the scene for the worst night of our lives. The road past our gate turned into a dirt track beyond our boundary, crossing our creek by means of an insecure wooden bridge and leading to the only property beyond ours. Ray, the far property's manager, was driving his 4WD home in the dark and the fog, too fast no doubt as was his habit, when Evans happened to be crossing the road. There was fog and dust and Ray didn't see him. A lighter car would have rolled but the 4WD, merciful in its own way, killed Evans instantly.

Ray came straight back to Willowmavin to tell us, almost in tears. He'd known Evans since he was small, knew he was now at large and guessed who it was that had sorted out his hay shed for him once or twice. He had cursed him, laughed at him and boasted in the Kilmore pub about him, for nobody else in the district was plagued by such a wombat. He said, 'I'll bury him for you. You won't want to see him.'

We would have buried him ourselves but as I said, that was the worst night of our lives and Evans death was submerged beneath other, even more dreadful things. I remember though the night before that, windless, starry and utterly normal, because it was then, the only time in my life, that I heard the Banshees. As I was going to bed I heard them, a thin, strange keening somewhere in the air outside, neither close nor distant but everywhere at once, as insistent as pain and as real. I remembered the sound next morning and by then I could guess what it must have been.

The Common Wombat

Vombatus Ursinus

This is the wombat species that we know best in Victoria, and have come to either love or hate according to our location and occupation. Its unpopularity among the farmers of eastern Victoria is understandable because of the damage it does to rabbit-wire fences by bulldozing its way through them, and to the land by its vigorous creation of burrows. In the western side of Victoria, where the habitat is not to its liking, it is a protected species. Subspecies inhabit Tasmania and Flinders Island, while its close relations, the Northern and Southern Hairy-nose wombats, now exist only in small, isolated areas of Queensland and south-western Australia respectively. Like so many of our native species the Hairy-nose wombat, probably because they live on the plains rather than in forested areas, have been no match for the advance of man over their habitat. In Queensland the Northern Hairy-nose wombat is almost extinct and only one tiny colony survives in a National Park.

The closest marsupial relation to the wombat is the koala and it is thought that about 25 million years ago they had a common ancestor. Even now they have a number of similar characteristics though one is arboreal and the other lives on the ground. In both cases their tails are almost non-existent, and they both have the same dental structure, a pair of incisors in both the lower and upper jaw but no canine teeth. These incisors are rootless and continue to grow throughout the animal's life. The wombat's lack of facial expression and his sedentary lifestyle have earned him a reputation for stupidity, but in fact the wombat's cerebral hemispheres are proportionately larger than in any other marsupial. Anyone who has associated closely with a wombat will find this quite believable, for inscrutable they may be but stupid they are not, and you discount their intellect and their determination at your own risk. A wombat with a goal in view stops for nothing, as any farmer with a wrecked fence will tell you.

Wombats in the wild breed all year round and mature females, who reach sexual maturity when they are two years old, will usually have a baby every year. The wombat's pouch faces backwards between the mother's hind legs, a sensible arrangement to save the baby being bombarded with earth when she digs. The female has two teats and the baby stays in the pouch on a teat for about six months, then follows close in its mother's footsteps for another ten or eleven months. Thereafter it lives the normal, solitary life of an adult, digging and sharing burrows within its territory. The motto of a wombat might well be, 'I keeps myself to myself' since it appears to feel no affection at all for its own kind except, during its early life, for its mother. Its home range may vary from about 5 to 25 hectares, depending on the availability of food, and on this there will be a number of burrows, some quite short but some more than 30 metres long, complex and complete with sleeping chambers. The wombats on the same range visit these burrows at random and may share them, but whether sleeping or grazing their attitude to other wombats is singularly indifferent, apart from the necessary chore of mating.

Daytime is sleeping time in summer and night is feeding time, with maybe a journey of two or three kilometres to find the best place to eat. In colder weather wombats often feed during the day to take advantage of the sun's warmth, since other than dogs and man there are no predators for an adult wombat to fear, and their feeding times are dictated by comfort rather than caution. Their diet consists of native grasses, herbs, sedges and the roots of trees and shrubs. This has led to certain male Australians being awarded the nickname of 'Wombat' because of their sexual habits, for a wombat, so it is said, 'Eats, roots and leaves.'

A wombat lives far longer in captivity than in the wild, perhaps for 20 years as opposed to 5 or 6, since he is in a secure environment and assured of adequate food. In the bush, even with the absence of predators and in spite of his size and weight, disease, malnutrition, motor cars, traps or bushfires may claim him. A mature wombat can weigh up to 40 kg, all of it bone and muscle, but there are still factors against which he has no defence. A common problem is sarcoptic mange, a mite-born and highly contagious disease that can spread through a whole area, eventually killing the affected animals in a slow and most unpleasant manner.

Tehree still has Griffiths, a wombat said to be of malign disposition, which I took down to her as a youngster perhaps 15 years ago. Since that time Griffiths has lived like a Lord and the only threats he has known have been issued by Griffiths himself against his devoted carers, yet even Griffiths has virtues. He has appeared, so I'm told, as Fatso in *A Country Practice* and I suspect that much of his aggression is tongue-in-cheek acting, or at worst a typical wombat tendency to bullying. Wombats are enigmatic characters, sometimes surly and rough but worthy of our respect and understanding.

Raising a baby wombat

Tehree's notes

'The rules for raising an orphaned baby wombat are much the same as those which apply to kangaroos and wallabies. Like them it will need a pouch until it is fully haired and weaned, round-the-clock feeding, cuddling and reassurance. You will need Wombaroo or Digestelac, and you will also need special wombat teats, obtainable from chemists who carry veterinary goods.

'When it starts to leave the pouch you will need a play-pen to confine it within civilised limits. When it's ready to go outside it'll need a pen in the garden, otherwise your garden will soon look like a bomb site, and it'll need roots and branches to chew on to help its teeth. Outside the pen it will follow you, nose-to-heel, wherever you go, and as it gets older its preferred sleeping place will turn out to be on your bed or your favourite armchair.

'The extent to which you and your household can develop genuine wombat-tolerance should not be tested too far, for the animal's sake as well as your own. Like the joeys, it will need to learn to do without blankets and tid-bits, so pass it on to a professional wildlife carer who will persuade it to be what nature meant it to be. Then, when your tears have dried after the parting, look round for another baby wombat to drive you mad.'

You would be forgiven for thinking that a koala who has nothing else to do spends the time practicing posing for a photograph.

6   Koalas

FEW PEOPLE are better qualified than Tehree to give koala wisdom to others. She has a constant koala population at Jirrahlinga which includes males and females, mothers with cubs, orphans, road victims, bushfire victims, invalids, convalescents and some permanent residents, unfit to return to the wild. There is nothing much she doesn't know about koalas, from infancy to old age

The koala has become a national symbol. Visit any Australian airport and you will find the gift shops piled high with fluffy koala replicas for the overseas visitors to take home to their children. The Japanese in particular find them irresistible. An Australian MP who dared to describe koalas as stupid, somnolent creatures that sleep in trees and piddle on humans from a great height, was lambasted in the press as if for blasphemy. His political career was probably damaged far more severely than if he'd made defamatory remarks about the British Monarchy or the Pope, yet to some extent he was correct. Being nocturnal animals koalas do spend most of the daytime sleeping, and since they have neither nappies nor portable toilets you stand underneath them at your own risk. However, few humans appear brilliant when they're fast asleep, and at night the koala is as active and intelligent as one could wish.

Similarly, the popular concept of a koala is of a furry, attractive but tediously inactive toy, permanently drunk on its diet of eucalyptus leaves and therefore lacking in personality. This is outrageously wrong. According to Tehree koalas have distinct personalities, different dietary and climatic preferences and a range of reactions to differing situations as wide and varied as our own might be. There are aggressive, self-opinionated koalas and humble, withdrawn characters, but unless you associate closely with them day and night, and few of us do, it's hard to appreciate their individuality.

Tehree's koala population fluctuates throughout the year. Recently she had twenty-four koalas in the Sanctuary, many of them rescued from bushfires in the Western District. Tehree is on call for Wildlife Rescue in bushfire emergencies all through the summer months, and she was in deep distress at what she had seen on her latest rescue mission. Arboreal animals such as koalas and possums are particularly vulnerable in bushfires. Compared with kangaroos, who have the speed to run in front of the fire, tree-dwellers are slow on the ground; in a fast-moving fire they have little chance but at least, unhindered, the chance is there, and miraculously some do survive. Tehree, searching the ash-covered forest floor for injured wildlife, came on the corpse of a koala. It had been making its run for safety when it hit a tangle of wire, dropped and left there by someone too idle to carry it away and the koala was trapped in it, unable to escape.

'Why can't people *think*?' Tehree said angrily. 'Why can't they realise what their trash can do if they leave it lying round? It's the same as fishing lines that we find round the necks of seals or birds, choking them, just because someone's too lazy to pick things up.'

Unfortunately very few people are as aware as Tehree of such possibilities. It seldom crosses the mind of a picnicker or a fisherman that his discarded junk might be lethal, yet it would be hard to find any Australian who doesn't profess pride in our wildlife and urge its protection.

A koala is particularly vulnerable to stress and when it decides that it can no longer cope with the trauma of a situation it can simply shut the world out, sink into a death sleep and never wake up. Tehree tells of a female koala which had recovered well enough from the Ash Wednesday fires to be released under the supervision of a Ranger friend in the You Yangs, the cluster of little mountains near Geelong. The Ranger promised to look after the koala until she was well established, but shortly after Tehree left her with him there was a violent electrical storm. The flare of lightning, the din of wind and thunder must have seemed to the koala like a renewal of the fires she'd recently survived.

'All the wildlife who'd been through the fires were terrified by that storm,' Tehree says. 'At Jirrahlinga some of them went into deep shock. The next day the Ranger in the You Yangs rang me and said he had some bad news, that the koala I'd taken to him had died in the night. I said I'd drive up and bring her back to bury her here, she'd been with us for quite a time and I'd become fond of her. He handed her to me when I arrived and she looked quite dead so I took her and started back to my car when I suddenly felt a movement, ever so slight, and realised she wasn't dead at all. It was the storm. She'd thought another fire had come and she'd gone into the death sleep.

'I knew that the only way to help her was to make her wake up and react to something positive, start living in the real world again. I took her to the local vet and we shook her and even slapped her until suddenly she took a swipe at us. The vet kept saying, "We medics just don't understand the koala's mentality." Then I drove her back to Jirrahlinga and for three days and nights we worked on her, took turns walking her and annoying her just to keep her from sinking back into her sleep. She got really angry with us but we kept her awake. In the end she suddenly decided to live, accepted some gum leaves and started eating.

'That storm showed us how deeply the fires had affected the wildlife and how strongly they remembered the wind and heat and noise. They'd all been through electrical storms before of course, but this one came too close to their recent fire terror. To give them a contrast to the storm noises we played soft classical music to them for days afterwards with tapes of the bushfire noises, taken from the ABC news bulletins of the fires, in the background. The sound of the music blotting out the fires seemed to help them.'

Because the koala is a unique animal the methods of helping them when they're injured and traumatised have had to be developed specially for that species. Some of Jirrahlinga's methods with koalas have been developed solely by Tehree, others by sharing experience with other Shelters or zoos. One of the fairly common problems is the koala with a broken arm or leg, impossible to put in a plaster cast because the koala must spend the convalescent period in a tree or the facsimile of a tree. Tehree has solved that by buying child-sized shorts made of the tight, Lycra-type material that cyclists ride in. For a broken leg she cuts a hole in the crutch which allows the animal's droppings and urine to escape, while the tight shorts prevent it from tearing at the bandages under them and help the setting of the bone. In the case of a broken arm she reverses the shorts and puts the crutch hole over the koala's head and its arms through the legs.

Koalas, like all injured animals, hate bandages and try to get them off as quickly as possible. Tehree says, 'When they have a wound that's been stitched it's no good putting bandages over the sutures and expecting them to stay there, the koala will tear the bandage off and scratch the stitches out. A lot of the koalas we get, especially the bushfire victims, have deep cuts or injured eyes and when the vet stitches them we get him to stitch a big button over the top of the sutures. That can stay there as long as it takes the wound to heal and the koala can't do anything about it because it is firmly stitched and it hurts if they try to pull it off. They get used to it and leave it alone. A koala covered with buttons looks a bit funny, but it works.

'People always think that when you get injured wildlife it's important to keep them in the dark. That's true for animals that are active in the daytime but with nocturnal animals like koalas and wombats, who are normally out and about at night, it's different. You need to make them think it's time for bed, so if at night time you leave the lights on, then they're more likely to rest.'

'When animals like koalas are hurt or traumatised it's important to keep them warm, just as you would with a person who's been injured or shocked. We've got imitation trees made of hollow pipes so that we can put hot water into the pipes and hang leaves around them. You'll see the koala feel that warmth when it's put onto the pipe-tree and its whole body relaxes, it can sit there and eat feeling safe and comfortable. Another thing is to get their feet warm because warmth comes from the feet upwards. We rub Vicks into the soles of their feet and put booties on them.'

Koalas are diligent mothers, and all koala cubs are accepted by the other females in the group and tolerated even when they're irritating, wanting to play and tease as all young things do. On the whole marsupial mothers have a far harder time than human mothers. They must house their babies on their stomachs for many months, even when they've become uncomfortably heavy, watch over them constantly whenever they leave the pouch and teach them everything they need to know. Try that routine on modern Australian mothers and our birth rate would have a spectacular fall, but wildlife carers, fostering orphaned babies, must do their best to replicate it.

For many years Tehree ran the Animal Nursery at the Royal Agricultural Show in Melbourne, bringing to town a selection of young animals so that children, and their parents, could see them and play with them. It was an enormously popular Show exhibit, very hard work for Tehree but, as she says, 'There's nothing to beat educating kids about animals when they're young. They could touch them in the Animal Nursery, instead of just seeing pictures of them in books.'

At the Royal Show of 1982 Tehree was raising a very young koala who was at the frequent bottle-feeding stage, so wherever she went the baby and its bottle went as well. One evening her mother, who was in Melbourne at the time, had been invited out to dinner by a gentleman friend, and Tehree was invited to join them. She was anxious to make a good impression, and rather than carry all her usual rather obtrusive feeding gear she put the tiny koala in her handbag with its bottle and towels. Once at the table she put her handbag, containing the tiny koala, on the floor beside her chair.

There was a large party at the table next to them and Tehree suddenly caught the sound of raised voices, a female voice shrill above the others.

'I saw it!' the voice cried. 'I tell you, I saw it! Just there!'

'Calm down, dear,' said a man's voice soothingly. 'You've just had a touch too much to drink, you're seeing things. Have a glass of water.'

Tehree decided it was no business of hers and returned to being a chaperone until there was another shriek, the same woman's voice in an even higher key. "THERE! I told you so! A KOALA!'

The baby was emerging from the handbag, Mickey Mouse ears tuned to the strange noises, bright and inquisitive. It had slept all day, and night, after all, is the time when young koalas wake up and take notice. Regardless of the restaurant lights the little animal's body clock said it was playtime.

Her mother's friend demanded to see the cause of the excitement, and Tehree's first thought was that he would not be at all happy about having his party disrupted. But he was delighted.

' I wish you'd bring that little thing along and show it to a young Scottish friend of mine who's visiting Australia. He'd love it.'

The friend was a man called Hamish Gordon, a tall, black-bearded Scot, ex show-jumper and polo player, lover of animals and with

Baby koala

ambitions to be a vet. Hamish was entranced by the baby koala, and Tehree invited him to come and help with the Animal Nursery at the Showgrounds. When the Show was over she lent him a car so that he could see something of the country, and before he left Australia he'd announced his intention of returning in a year's time to marry her. In the event he left Australia in October and came back to marry Tehree just three months later.

Tehree reckons that if she had taken a baby wombat to the dinner and on to her first meeting with Hamish, the relationship might have ended there and then, because Hamish is antipathetic to wombats. This always strikes me as strange, since many Scots and wombats share a taciturn, enigmatic personality and Hamish should feel at home with them. In any case, it was not a wombat, but a koala. Not many koalas earn the name of Cupid, but it could well have fitted the restaurant baby.

Koalas can turn up in unexpected places. As human habitation spreads outwards from the towns into the bushland you may get an 'urban koala', the stray who appears unaccountably in some outer-suburban backyard, and the chances are that it is searching for a remembered feeding site which has now become a building block. Tehree has had a number of calls from householders asking her to remove such visitors, one from a resident who complained of a koala 'walking up and down outside the windows, staring in at us. The poor thing must be somebody's pet.'

'The house must have been on the koala's old range,' Tehree said. 'It was peering through the windows looking for the trees. Animals and birds don't understand glass.' This koala was lucky to be collected before it came to any harm, for the urban scene is full of dangers. Dogs, cars and swimming pools are all potential killers. While the koala may wander in through an open gate, a solid, unclimbable fence such as Colorbond can trap it, and a koala that falls into a swimming pool will be unable to climb out and must drown.

'People who live in the outer suburbs should leave a thick rope with one end securely fixed outside their pool, the other end with a big knot in it lying in the water' says Tehree. 'A koala will grab it and pull itself out. I know a woman who had two koalas drown in her swimming pool and finally put one of these ropes in and it was just as well, because her three-year-old granddaughter saved herself with it. She fell into the pool and was able to hang onto the rope and call for help.

'It's important to know how to handle a koala, for your sake as well as theirs. If you hit one with your car and are taking it to a Shelter or a vet, prop it up so that it's sitting as it would in a tree. It will die if you lie it down. And if you have to catch one, always pick it up from behind so that it can't scratch or bite you.

'I'll give you a good example of what can go wrong. My friend Joan and I were on our way back to Jirrahlinga one day when we saw a bunch of people on the road. They'd all got out of their cars and were staring at a big koala. He may have been hit by a car and hurt or just dazed, but nobody seemed to be actually doing anything about it. Joan went to see if she could help and I went to get a blanket out of our car. There was one man who was the kind of know-all you always get in these situations and I heard him say to Joan, "It's okay, I know all about these little fellers. Stand back, I'll just pick 'im up, put 'im in my ute and run 'im down to the vet." I knew there was a good wildlife vet nearby so it made sense.

'Then Joan said, "I'd use a blanket to pick him up if I were you, you might get bitten," but this wise guy said "Listen, lady! I know what I'm doing and I don't need no blanket. You just grab 'em by the scruff and the bum, like this…"

'I could see the koala's body language and knew there was going to be trouble and Joan could see it too so she shouted "Look out!" but it was too late. As he swung the koala up it grabbed him by the balls with one hand, sank the claws of a foot into his leg and hung on as hard as it could. Joan didn't offer to help and the other people didn't seem too keen to help either. He was dancing around with tears in his eyes and I put a blanket over the koala's head so that at least it wouldn't bite him. I said, "Stop jumping about, you're scaring the koala to death." When we'd finally separated the two of them he saw the notice, Wild Life Rescue Service, on the side of our car, but he didn't seem too grateful.

'Sometimes you'll get koalas who climb up telegraph poles. People get frightened that they'll touch the wires and be electrocuted so they try to grab them from below. You can't do that to a koala, it'll go upwards straight away and be electrocuted for sure, besides which you'll put the whole district out of power. You've got to get above it and force it down with a hand on its head until it's low enough for someone to grab it.'

This is all useful koala wisdom, and though the average city-dweller may never even see a grey furry backside high above him in the treetops, it's handy to know. The unexpected does sometimes happen, and this is a national icon, not just a pretty toy.

If you visit Jirrahlinga, you can meet him in person, touch him, talk to him and begin to know who he really is.

The Koala

Phascolarctos cinereus
The koala is the only surviving member of an ancient family, though scientists believe that about 25 million years ago it shared a common

ancestor with the wombat. The koala has come a long way from the wombat since then, to the top of the tree so to speak, not only in terms of habitat but also as one of the world's favourite animals, whereas Cousin Wombat scarcely rates a mention at home or abroad. Because the koala is virtually defenceless the fortunes of the species have seesawed over the years, always at the mercy of factors outside its control. Before ever the white man arrived they were a favourite, easily accessed food item, both for the Aborigines who took them from the trees and for dingoes which caught them on the ground, and the koala population was under constant pressure. As Europeans developed the country for agriculture and grazing the situation changed. War was declared on dingoes and their numbers declined, while many Aborigines became urbanised and acquired a taste for European food. The koala population increased until, at the end of the 19th century, the enlightened newcomers to Australia found it profitable to hunt the harmless creatures for their skins.

A female koala will accept and tolerate babies belonging to other koalas.

Now they are totally protected but their habitat steadily declines, forcing them into limited areas where they may be subject to disease or an inadequate food supply through overcrowding. Government conservation authorities move koalas from one area to another to rectify this, but frequently the new sites are unsuitable, or there is a lack of supervision after the move to ensure that the transfer has been successful. Koalas may have fewer predators these days but we have presented them with new dangers against which they have no more defence than against dingoes or human hunters.

Koalas feed on no less than seventeen varieties of eucalypt, their stomach being uniquely designed for the digestion of a food that would be totally inedible for most other species. The belief that eucalyptus leaves keep koalas in a permanent drunken stupor is a myth, but it is not a diet that produces a lot of energy. The koala must eat a great many leaves in order to have enough energy to find more leaves, a Catch 22 situation which explains its habitual immobility during non-eating hours. At night they move from one tree to another in search of fresh food, play, mate and do all the things that other animals do by day. They may travel for some distance on the ground, searching for new food trees, but they stick to the forested areas; it is rare to find a koala in open country where instinct tells it there is danger from predators. Farming has therefore created new problems for them. The practice of leaving patches of woodland widely separated by open paddocks means that they may eat out one patch and starve, afraid to move to another feeding site without the cover of a corridor of trees.

Tehree tells of a colony of koalas, established in an area close to Warrnambool, which increased to the point where the animals were starving. It was on land shared by an Aboriginal community and she spoke to one of the tribal elders there. 'It is white man's problem,' he said. The colony had been established by the conservation authorities in a place where there were no tree corridors, so the koalas, though increasing in number, were unable to move to other feeding grounds.

The daytime habitat of the koala is in a eucalypt, his bottom resting snugly in a fork of the tree, his hands grasping a branch and his eyes closed in restorative sleep. His hands are 'split', the first two digits opposed to the other three so that in climbing he can get a grip on tree trunks or branches, while the first toe of his hind feet helps in upward traction. Both fore and hind feet are equipped with effective claws, a factor to be borne in mind if you pick up a wild koala: always do so from behind to avoid being clawed or bitten. A male Victorian koala can weigh 12 or 13 kg and a swipe delivered in fear or anger is no joke.

Although koalas live in colonies they are essentially solitary animals, moving about at night within their range and travelling appreciable distances between food trees. Their method of travel on the ground is quadrupedal using both fore and hind limbs, efficient enough in normal circumstances but not very fast, so that in bushfires or pursued by a predator they're extremely vulnerable.

In captivity, as in the koala compound at Jirrahlinga, they live at much closer quarters than in the wild and interact very amicably, but this may be because there is no need to compete for food. In the bush a congregation of koalas in one food tree would soon strip it bare, and a wise animal keeps its tree to itself.

The ability of the koala to live on its eucalyptus leaf diet is one of its most remarkable features. The leaves contain phenolic compound, strong smelling oils and even cyanide precursors, a mixture that would certainly poison any other creature that tried to digest it. The koala's stomach has adapted itself by forming the largest caecum of any marsupial, and in this caecum microbial fermentation occurs, while the liver detoxifies the oils and phenolic compounds. The leaves are high in fibre, low in protein and energy production, but they have the virtue of containing water so that in normal circumstances the koala doesn't need to drink.

The male koala is larger than the female and both have sternal glands, the male's bigger than the female's and used for scent marking by rubbing the chest against a tree, a deterrent to rival males in the breeding season. The female koala becomes sexually mature at 2 years and thereafter usually has one cub a year, but rarely twins. Unlike the kangaroo the koala has only two teats in her pouch which, like the wombat's pouch, faces backwards between her hind legs. The baby, only weighing 0.5 g at birth must climb into the pouch from the urogenital opening, but unlike the kangaroo both the koala and wombat babies have only a short distance to go. The newborn koala stays in the pouch on one nipple for 7 months and in the last pouch month the mother begins weaning the cub. In the beginning she feeds it soft faeces from her caecum, apparently to inoculate it with the micro-organisms which will allow its own caecum to function on a eucalypt diet. During weaning the cub graduates to a mixed diet of leaves and milk, spending time outside the pouch and travelling on its mother's back, clamped to her fur like a small rucksack.

By the time the cub is a year old it is fully weaned, becomes independent of its mother and will leave her, a disadvantage compared with the young kangaroo which stays with the herd and gets a full education by example. During the period between first separation and true adulthood there is a high mortality rate among the young, ignorant koalas who must learn the ways of a hostile world on their own. In the bad old days of multiple predators, the dingoes and hunters, their chances of survival must have been very slim. Though many of the threats to the koala's existence have been removed, others are growing with the logging of the eucalypt forests and the clearing of land for grazing both isolating and reducing koala habitat. Given wise and sympathetic management our koalas will survive, but their future is now in our hands.

Raising a baby koala

Tehree's notes

'In my experience baby koalas, like all marsupials at the pouch stage, need attention round the clock. If they were in the pouch of their natural mother they'd know only her warmth and her smell, so at Jirrahlinga we try to duplicate that. If we get a "pinkie" koala one of our keepers takes it over, carries it all day and sleeps with it at night. They're asked not to change their perfume, if they use it, their shampoo, their soap or anything that might give them an unfamiliar scent. There was a vet who laughed at this routine, but by the time he'd checked on the progress of three baby koalas raised that way he stopped laughing. Yes, they're allowed to wash and change their clothes, as this doesn't add a new scent. In fact, we're fussy about such things at Jirrahlinga.

'There are a number of formulas you can get for feeding baby

It's good to share things with friends..

....but better still if you have one each.

koalas, Prosebee, Wombaroo or Divetelac, double strength. This last product was recommended by Dr Rosemary Booth, a well-known wildlife vet at Healesville Sanctuary. As they get older we use what we call Koala Glug, a mixture of gum leaves and a substitute for pap which is made from a mix of gum leaves and healthy koala faeces. It helps their gut flora when they start feeding on eucalyptus leaves.

'Koala babies that have been bottle-raised are as keen on their bottle as any other young animal, human babies included. A friend of mine brought her baby son round one day when we had a young koala, just being weaned, in the house. It walked into the room where the little kid was drinking from his bottle, saw it and walked up to him. The baby pointed the bottle towards the koala who must have thought it was being offered to him, so it grabbed it from the baby and started sucking. We gave the koala a feeding bottle with his own formula in it and they both sat there, drinking from bottles in the same chair.

'Like all pouch animals baby koalas want to go on suckling from their mother after they leave the pouch and start on solid food. Their heads get quite large, and even when their bodies can't fit into the pouch any longer they'll force their heads into it to get at the teat, until their mother gets fed up and chases them off. Kangaroo joeys often do this when there's actually a young brother or sister suckling in the pouch, but the older joey always uses the teat he started life on. By that time his special teat has been elongated, pulled out of shape by his sucking, and it wouldn't be any good to the new baby who's had to go onto a teat that fits into its mouth.

'We've fostered an orphaned koala baby onto a mother who lost her own cub. She'd been hit by a car and the baby in her pouch was so badly damaged it had to be put down. At the same time Dr Booth had a baby whose mother had died, and the unfurred baby was almost the same age as the one we'd lost. While one of the staff went to Healesville to get the baby we managed to get milk from our lactating mother, and when the orphan arrived we put it in her pouch. We watched it all night. It detached itself from the teat twice and we were able to give it supplementary feeds of the foster mother's milk. Both of them did well and when the young koala was almost independent they were released in the Otways. It's easier to get a female koala to accept these orphaned babies at the unfurred, suckling stage than when they're about six months old, but for some reason they'll accept a hand reared youngster after it's finished suckling.

'The young koala needs a nursery tree when he starts to get independent of his carer, a small tree on a stand with leaves attached and a cuddle-toy that he can climb on. That way he'll gradually progress to climbing real trees. And remember, by the way, if you have a young koala in the house don't go off and leave him alone in a room. They're very inquisitive and you'll probably find the room wrecked when you come back.

'When we get injured koalas brought to us I don't put them into a dark room and isolate them, I try to simulate daylight which is the time when they sleep. They need an environment as near as possible to their own, so in the koala hospital there are small birds twittering nearby and other koalas as well. We have a recipe for these injured and stressed koalas to improve their body condition, a mash of steamed pumpkin and sometimes a steamed apple. We keep a quantity of this mixture frozen for situations like fires or floods but frozen food loses its goodness once it's thawed, and for koalas that are dehydrated and debilitated I add a Berocca tablet. It's good for humans with a hangover and after all, what's that but dehydration?

'The other thing we use a lot for dehydration is Hartmann's fluid, the same thing that's given by intravenous drip in hospital. We take it on bushfire rescues and it's obviously impossible to give it to an animal by drip in the bush so we give it orally, directly into the mouth. Vets and students are horrified when I tell them this, but it works. I've given it to koalas, possums and wallabies at a fire scene and they all survived. It's standard practice now for our rescue team to carry Hartmann's and in fact all dehydrated birds and animals get it, birds by a special syringe that delivers it directly into their crop.

'Always remember how susceptible koalas are to stress. Don't let your children look on them as playmates they can treat roughly or shout at and don't let your dogs chase them. If you live in koala country wild ones may visit your garden, so have a rope in your swimming pool and a garden fence they can climb over if they get shut in.

'Unless a koala's in trouble enjoy it, respect it and leave it alone.'

7 Possums

YOU DON'T HAVE TO LIVE in the country to know about possums. The fantasy about kangaroos in our city streets once made us famous abroad, but nobody seems to think it remarkable that our city streets and gardens are alive with possums. Our relationship with city possums is ambivalent at best, although they live closer to us than any other of our wildlife species. We can ignore the millions of truly rural possums who never come near a town, but the urban brigade is too conspicuous to be overlooked, and an animal that should be enjoyed is often detested. This is a sad situation, because with a little understanding and co-operation on our part we could live happily with our garden possums. They are, after all, the only one of all our wildlife species that shows any desire to share our personal space, and we should regard it as a compliment.

There are dedicated Possum People, of course, people who appreciate them and try to make their lives easier, by providing food and shelter for the disadvantaged and suitable release for the evicted. At Jirrahlinga Tehree cares for injured possums, raises an orphanage-full of babies each year and releases them strictly out of town. Ninon Phillips, the wildlife artist and carer who gave me my first introduction to Tehree, is another card-carrying Possum Lady. Ninon has a lovely, old and rambling brick house in Hawthorn, one of those houses which speak of times past and gracious living. Today the greater part of its high-ceilinged interior is animal and bird accommodation, cages stacked on cages, bird calls, squeaks and grunts the music that fills its halls. Ninon is no longer young, her hair is white and at times wild, but she administers her urban Shelter with the skill of a small, resourceful general directing his troops, and defence of possums is her personal mission.

At the height of her possum-caring career her nights were devoted to bread-distribution in Melbourne's parks in the company of volunteer helpers, and possums are always prominent among the occupants of the cages in her home. Ninon's possums are finally released in suitable areas far from town, since otherwise they will return whence they came. The professional possum catcher, to whom time is money, may remove the possums from your garden but then release them within a relatively short distance, or in an unsuitable area. If they are released within the possum's navigation range, which is impressively large, they will return to their favourite garden like homing pigeons. If another possum family hasn't already moved in the householder, who regards possums as the Eighth Plague of Egypt and has paid the possum catcher good money to remove them, finally has them eradicated in ways that are not always nice.

Possums arouse a whole range of emotions and misconceptions in the minds of the Australian public, from the people who genuinely like them and want them around to those who regard them as inherently savage, evil and destructive. Those who like and encourage them should learn a little possum-sense to keep the relationship under control. The truth is that possums are only too ready to take human handouts, and if a well-disposed householder encourages them with nightly food and soft words they see no reason to let the friendship end there. 'This is a cushy situation,' they say to themselves. 'What is theirs is obviously ours, they are generous, good-hearted people and they want us to be happy.' Over-encouragement can lead to misunderstandings, and if you want to enjoy the possums in your garden you must arrange things so that they know their place.

For a start, cover the tops of your chimneys with wire mesh so that they can't climb down them, and have your house possum-proofed so that they can't get into the ceiling. Don't plan your garden with an expensive rose bed as the centre- piece because the possums will assume you've done it for their benefit and react accordingly, also net your fruit trees and cover your vegetable patch with wire mesh. When, after dusk, you indulge in the undoubted pleasure of calling them down from the trees and feeding them, give them food suitable for possums, bread or fruit but not human food such as cake or chocolate, and always feed them in a special place, well-removed from your house.

As an example, Tehree was woken at one o'clock one morning by a phone call. 'The woman who called was in a terrible state, she'd been woken up by what she described as "a furry animal eating some chocolate they'd left beside the bed." She'd frightened the possum so that it had leapt to the floor and taken off somewhere in the bedroom. "I can't go to sleep with that creature in the room," she said. "Come and help me, please!"

'It didn't sound to me like a very threatening situation and I was tired so I suggested that her husband might throw a towel over it and put it outside, but she said her husband was out. I said "How about a neighbour?" and she said she knew her neighbour's wife was out, and she couldn't risk the gossip if the man came over at that hour. I thought about sending Hamish but heaven knows what trouble that might have caused, a tall, dark, bearded stranger, so I said I'd go. I told her to turn on all the lights and shut the bedroom door so the possum couldn't get out. She didn't shut the door, of course, and it took us ages to find the possum but it suddenly dashed out from under a sofa, between the woman's legs and up a curtain. She let out such a scream that her neighbour called the police who turned up and found that everything was fine, the possum caged and covered with a towel and this woman quite happy again. I went out on the policeman's arm. He was a man I knew and I thought it would give the neighbours a bit more to talk about.'

'The possum was so tame when I got it back to Jirrahlinga that I thought it must have been hand-raised as a pet and I rang the woman to tell her it was fine. She said it hadn't actually been hand-raised but that she'd been putting out food on the barbecue table every night. I asked her what she'd been feeding it and she admitted she'd given it chocolate biscuits. "Was your bedroom window open?" I asked, and she said, "Yes." That explained it, the little possum had smelled the chocolate by her bed and thought it had been invited in to help itself.

'I took the possum back with a possum nesting-box. We make them at Jirrahlinga. I fixed the box on a tree with a food tray underneath, and told the woman what to feed it and always to put the food on the feeding tray. As far as I know they've been living together happily ever since.

'You get the other end of the stick, people who are really scared of possums. There was a time when I was called to a boarding house in one of those elite Geelong schools. The maintenance manager said they'd found a mother possum and a baby behind one of the gas fires that had been placed in under a chimney, and what should they do? I told him to pull the gas fire out, put a cloth over the mother and baby and release them outside, then put a wire cover over the chimney. It didn't seem to me like a problem for a maintenance manager but he wasn't what you'd call a brave man.

'"No way!" he said. "They can tear your arms off, those things, rip you to pieces. I'm not going near it and we can't ask the boys to do it. What about health and safety? What about insurance? You'll have to come. We'll even make a donation to your Sanctuary!" By the time he'd rung me twice more I decided I'd better go. I caught the mother and her baby but I was horrified to find the skeletons of almost a dozen Brushtails in the fireplace where the gas fire had been. They'd fallen down the chimney which was built so that they couldn't get back up, and starved to death There must have been a lot of noise and a terrible smell, but nobody had thought to look.

'Lots of people are paranoid about Brushtails. I remember a workman describing the horrible animals he'd found in the wall of a house that was being renovated, "They're big, abut the size of a dog, with a big, black tail and huge teeth and they hold up their paws like boxing gloves!" He wasn't game to go near them. Funnily enough there were fifteen possums living in the wall cavities there, and they're supposed to be solitary animals. It just shows what they'll do if accommodation's provided for them.

'When possums get into your roof it's no good just removing them, or having them removed and thinking that's the end of the problem. The possum smell will still be there, so other possums will decide it's legitimate possum habitat and move in. The roof cavity must be sprayed with Nilodour and sealed so that it's no longer an attraction to other squatter-possums.

'It always amazes me that so many people move into beautiful treed areas and then complain about the wildlife. They plant things like roses and fruit trees in their gardens and wonder why they get eaten. They ask me, "How can I get rid of these possums that are ruining my garden?" and I ask them why they bought a house in a wildlife area if they couldn't live with the wildlife. They don't realise that in that kind of setting, if you get rid of one lot of possums, all the other possums in the district will be fighting to take their place. If you're going to live in the bush you should plan your life and your garden to fit in with the wild creatures, then you can enjoy them. After all, they were there first.'

It's true that Brushtails are habitually more aggressive than the smaller and to my mind enchanting Ringtail possum who, apart from a dietary obsession with roses, fruit and other valued garden products, has few vices. A hand-raised Brushtail can become as tame as any other hand-raised marsupial but in time he will become explicitly what he was meant to be, a wild animal. Like all possums he's an opportunistic feeder and ready enough to climb down a tree after dark to take food from your hand, but don't attempt to stroke him. Give him bread and respect, then you can enjoy each other's company.

A Ringtail possum, on the other hand, can become the most beguiling, affectionate pet and companion you will ever know, though he too will eventually want his freedom. Take, for example, Samson. He came to us because he fell out of his nest as many baby possums do, and was lucky enough to be picked up by someone with a conscience. He got the name Samson because though he fitted easily into the palm of my hand he was a warrior from the start, a keen feeder who gripped the eye-dropper and sucked long after he'd had enough, his tummy round and shiny as a well-filled chestnut. When he graduated to independent locomotion he simply took over the house, the dogs and cats and particularly the kitchen where he liked to supervise and test the cooking. Confinement traumatised him. The most commodious possum accommodation was provided but he simply curled himself into a ball of misery and refused to eat. He was too young to release so we surrendered, apologised and let him live free in the house.

Samson's main drawback was that having a lusty appetite for food and drink he also had a lusty pee. Anyone who has had possums in their roof will know that possum-pee not only smells bad but it leaves a horrendous stain. I began to watch Samson obsessively, knowing that when he squatted, spread his hind legs and stiffened his tail a pee would surely follow. As soon as the signs appeared I'd grab him, rush him to the sink and hold him over the plughole until he'd finished, at the same time telling him what a brilliant, talented fellow he was. It took him very little time to catch on and thereafter he'd come hurtling from the furthest reaches of the house, over the kitchen

Releasing a brushtail possum

bar and into the sink where he'd pee tidily down the plughole, his face saying quite clearly, 'A near thing, but I made it!'

As he grew older we fed him only his natural food and let him go in and out of an open window at night. There were plenty of other Ringtails around; we saw them in the garden, heard them and noted their addiction to our roses. Samson was bound to meet them in their natural element of darkness, would be drawn gradually to his own kind rather than to us and eventually he'd join them. Just as we'd hoped he began to stay out all night, returning at daylight to sleep curled up on one of my jumpers, then a period of days and nights would pass without a sign of him and finally he ceased to come home at all. Like all wildlife releases it was satisfaction and loss and the worry of wondering. Predators wait out there for small possums and one will never know for sure, but at least he had a chance to live the life he was meant to live and perhaps, with the help of the God of Small Things, he prospered.

Possums are a much-maligned species. In their natural habitat of the bush they do no harm at all, merely serving their particular purpose in the scheme of things. Man, in creating his own urban environment, failed to understand that in doing so he was also providing the perfect form of easy living for possums. The average well-treed and flowered suburban garden, convenient living space in the house roof not to mention well filled dustbins, add up to possum heaven and we can hardly blame them for making use of the free benefits we thoughtfully provide. Nor should we complain when, having been removed to not-so-distant parts, at considerable expense by a professional possum catcher, they doggedly make their way back to the Promised Land.

The Common Brushtail Possum

Trichosurus vulpocura

The Brushtail possum is bigger, brasher, meaner and more macho than the Ringtail. He even belongs to a different family, and is widely distributed throughout eastern and southern Australia and Tasmania, Central Australia and south western Australia. His cousin, the Cuscus, inhabits New Guinea and comes no further south than Cape York.

The natural habitat of the Brushtail is among the lower branches of the forests although science cautiously admits the obvious, that he 'cohabits with humans.' This, being translated, means that the thunderous footsteps in the ceiling which ruin your sleep are the work of a cohabiting Brushtail. Equally, although his diet is supposed to be confined to leaves and fruit, the wreckage round your dustbins indicates that he has learned to appreciate a variety of different foods, tastier than eucalyptus leaves and easier to digest. His voice is almost as intrusive as his footsteps overhead, a loud guttural cough and a prolonged hiss which advertises his territory to other males and his presence to females in the breeding season. His other tools for territorial establishment are his scent glands, under the chin, on the chest and near the anus.

Brushtails have a high birth rate, breeding mainly in autumn, less commonly in spring, but births have been recorded all year round. The females begin to reproduce when they're only a year old, some of them breeding twice in the year. Unlike the Ringtail they have only one baby, less than three weeks after mating, and carry it in their pouch for four to five months. During the weaning period of one to two months the young continue to suckle but spend most of their time riding on their mothers' backs. When they leave their mothers to make their own way in life the mortality rate is very high, especially among the males who subsequently make up only a third of the population. All carnivores, foxes, dingoes and domestic dogs appreciate a meal of young possum meat, and although they are principally arboreal Brushtails frequently take to the ground where they are easy prey. Being nocturnal they spend the daytime in a den, a hollow tree, a dead branch or a fallen log but do not build a nest as the Ringtail does, neither do they have the same climbing advantage of a hand with opposing fingers nor the fully prehensile tail. Their hind feet, however, have an opposing first toe and this, as well as their sharp claws and to some extent their tails, make them efficient climbers, able to jump between branches in search of food. Their size and colour vary according to their location, from copper-coloured and short-haired in Queensland to dark and woolly in the cold climate of Tasmania.

This adaptability to location means that they can colonise and survive in almost any forested area. In 1840 we copied the people who imported our own foreign pests by introducing the Brushtail possum to New Zealand where it has become a national curse, thriving in the Kiwi forests and systematically destroying them. The New Zealand possums are hunted for their pelts, and the possum skin industry is a healthy contributor to the economy. We hunted them for their skins in Australia in the past, but now they are protected on the mainland and partly protected in Tasmania.

The Common Ringtail Possum
Pseudocheirus peregrinus
In Victoria we're lucky enough to have a large number of these small, sociable possums, and they also occur in populations of varying size from the tip of Cape York to Tasmania and in the south west of Western Australia. Their tail, which gave them their name, is white tipped and tightly curled like a watch spring when not in use for climbing, jumping among branches or carrying nesting material, a functional fifth limb. Wrap their tail round your finger and they can hang from it, then turn and climb up it like a rope, or swing from a branch by it to reach the most succulent food. Like the koala their hands are designed for climbing with the first and second fingers opposing the other three fingers, giving a perfect grip on a branch. The Ringtail likes to live in dense, tangled foliage and to build its spherical, lined, bark and grass nest in a hollow tree or some other safe camouflage.

They breed between April and November, carry their young in the pouch for about four months and wean them at six months. The mother has four teats and usually has only two young, but Tehree was once brought a female that had been killed by a cat and found four babies in her pouch. This would have been a terrible burden for the mother, before and during their weaning when they would all have expected to ride on her back. In such multiple birth situations in their wild state the weaker young are seldom allowed to survive, but are pushed from the nest.

Ringtail possums are strictly nocturnal, most often abroad in the early part of the night, and although they do not form permanent groups they socialise, sharing their nesting sites and home ranges. They vocalise, but unlike the noisier Brushtail possum their cry is a

The white possum box provides accommodation for a pair of Ringtail possums. Both are at home, as can be seen from a count of tails.

soft, twittering call, more like the voice of a bird than an animal. The feral cat is their worst predator in the wild and the domestic cat in urban areas, since they can hunt in the high branches where the Ringtail lives. Birds of prey such as the Wedgetail eagle and the larger raptors hunt them too, while loss of the trees themselves, through logging and land clearing by man, is their long-term threat. The least we can do, in view of the danger we create for this most lovely animal, is to welcome him into our gardens, and to turn a blind eye on the odd, stolen rose.

The Sugar Glider

Pretaurus breviceps

Somewhere in the distant past a population of the Ringtail's ancestors, already adept at leaping between branches, decided that it would be even better if they could glide between the trees. Over time these little marsupials have developed a membrane which stretches between their front and hind legs, so that when they push themselves from a tree, limbs outstretched, they became a kind of miniature flying carpet. The Sugar glider, a medium-size member of the glider clan and a common inhabitant of Victorian woodlands, can glide for at least 50 metres and land, soft as featherdown, exactly where it wants to land. Flight enables it to exploit quite widely separated food trees as well as protecting it from predators. Its relationship to the Ringtail possum is obvious at a glance in spite of the glider's white-edged flight membrane, lighter colour and smaller size because they have the same head shape, huge, luminous eyes and pricked ears. The Sugar glider's flying membrane stretches from the fifth finger of the hand to the first toe of the hind foot, a decorative, soft-furred ruffle except in flight.

Tehree has bred Sugar gliders at Jirrahlinga and says that, like the Ringtail, they can become very friendly.

'I had one called Pippin who'd come when I called him. He'd fly onto my shoulder, or sometimes land on my head which was a bit disconcerting if you weren't expecting it, but he loved people, even strangers and especially blind people. That was amazing; he wouldn't let sighted strangers touch him but he'd let blind people 'look at him' all over with their hands. He lived in our house until he was nine years old, then one morning I heard him calling me, which was unusual. I got out of bed to see what was the matter and he came to my shoulder, curled up under the collar of my dressing gown and ten minutes later he was dead. He knew he was going to die, and I felt privileged that he'd chosen to die like that.

'Sugar gliders are very easily stressed and they suffer terribly after bushfires when their trees are gone, the leaves are burnt and the whole landscape is strange and alien. Birds of prey always hang round after fires, looking for an easy meal and these little gliders are exposed to them, utterly defenceless. They suffer burns and inhalation damage as well. In the wild they live in groups of about seven adults and their young, sharing a common nest. After the Ash Wednesday fires, when we saved a lot of them, we kept them in little groups and released them as groups into the areas they'd come from. Some of them had seemed to recognise each other immediately and there's no reason why they wouldn't have done well together in the bush.'

Sugar gliders recognise each other by smell, exuded by scent-marking glands. In Victoria the breeding season begins in August and the female produces two infants which stay in the pouch for about seventy days, then graduate to the group nest for another thirty days. After that they leave the nest with their mother to learn to forage. Most of the young animals leave their original groups when they are seven to ten months old and travel to other forest areas, either joining other established groups or forming new ones with other juveniles. They are by no means cowardly, and will defend a food source with vigour against a Brushtail. Their call, usually a warning, is a shrill, yapping sound.

There are other varieties of glider in different areas of Victoria but the Sugar glider is by far the most common. As a baby it is easily mistaken for the young of an endangered species, the Leadbeater's possum. I made that mistake myself once, with dramatic results. I rang the Conservation Department to say that a nest of possible Leadbeater's babies had been chopped down in a tree near Kilmore, that I'd retrieved one of the little ones but that others had been given to people in the district and was the Department interested?

Within an hour quiet night-time Kilmore was full of police cars with flashing lights, escorting uniformed Department Rangers avid to track down the missing treasures. They finally converged on our Stud, sundry policemen and a large, frantic Ranger carrying on a cloth another of the babies, fully five inches long. Almost in tears he was trying to give it mouth to mouth resuscitation and nearly blowing its head off. In the excitement my baby escaped from its box and disappeared under the furniture. My husband, using four letter words, locked himself in his office, the Ranger's baby died of understandable stress and we finally ran mine to earth under the sofa. They turned out to be Sugar gliders, and it took me a long time to live my mistake down.

Raising a baby possum or Sugar glider

Tehree's notes

'If the baby you find is furless it must have warmth immediately, even before you go to a vet or wildlife carer for help. The best way is to wrap it in something soft and put it inside your clothes, next to your skin. This is the nearest you can get to the constant warmth of its mother's pouch and, in case you're squeamish, it won't do you any harm. Go and get help though, there are many varieties of possums and gliders and it's most important that you find out the correct food for the one you've rescued. It will need fluid, water or rehydration fluid to begin with until you find out the right formula, but not cow's milk.

'If you don't feed a young animal the correct food for its species you may make it ill or even kill it, so this is another reason for getting expert help. Possums and gliders may feed on native bushes, eucalyptus leaves, fruits, moths, grubs, beetles or larvae and you've got to know which is right for their particular species. When you get a baby home give it something soft and warm to snuggle into or under, keep it in a warm place without draughts and leave it quiet until you can get help. The animal will certainly be stressed and they can all die of stress; it may seem quiet and cuddly but you'll make things worse by handling it.

'When it's reared and weaned it will have to be released, and you should take advice about this from a wildlife carer. As with all other wild species, a wrongly managed release can be fatal.'

8   Monotremes

The Echidna

Tachyglossus aculeatus

The echidna or Spiny ant eater is an amiable character, a threat to no-one except the ants he feeds on. Since no other form of wildlife shares his consuming passion for ants he's non-competitive, and the other bush residents either ignore him or regard him as a friend. As an example, one warm, sunny day I got out of a 4WD on top of a stony hill in central Tasmania. There was a very large black Tasmanian tiger snake, asleep and neatly coiled a few feet away and resting in the exact middle of its coils, also asleep, was a large echidna. They made a touching picture and I'm sorry that I had no camera. The snake saw me first and uncoiled himself at high speed so that the echidna, landing with a thump on the ground, stared round in astonishment, saw me and rolled himself into Defence Position No.1. The tiger snake headed under the nearest rock and I couldn't help wondering whether their previous position had been a matter of mutual affection, negotiation or accident.

The Short-beaked echidna, together with the Long-beaked which lives in Papua New Guinea, have the distinction of being members of the order *Monotremata*. The only other member of this order is the platypus and the term *monotreme*, which means 'one hole,' refers to the single opening through which both faeces and urine are voided and through which the female also lays her eggs. The male echidna has the essential addition of a penis to enable him to mate and, like the platypus, a spur on the hind leg, but the echidna's spur is not attached to a venom gland.

Male echidnas have a well-developed but also well-controlled libido, since in the mating season, July through August, females have been seen being followed by up to six males. This is known as an Echidna Train and they proceed solemnly in single file, politely waiting their turn. The female lays one soft-shelled egg a year, curling herself into a ball so that her one, all-purpose opening deposits the egg into a fold of skin on her stomach where it hatches after ten days. This skin-fold is often referred to as a pouch because it serves the same purpose, protection and temperature-control for the egg, safe haven and feeding quarters for the baby while it grows. The echidna has no nipples but exudes milk through ducts on her abdomen, and the baby lives in her pouch/skin-fold feeding from these ducts for three months, by which time it has grown a covering of small spines.

The juvenile echidnas do not appear in public until they are about a year old, around November or December, and during these months the mother and her offspring spend their time in a burrow or some other private spot, concentrating on weaning and education.

Echidnas live mainly on ants and termites, their beak housing a long tongue covered with sticky saliva which they can insert into anywhere an ant can live. Given a solid, earthen ant hill it uses both claws and beak to make an opening, then devours the residents. Monotremes are toothless, so both the platypus with his duckbill and the echidna with his highly efficient tongue have developed feeding tools appropriate to their diet. The echidna masticates his food between two horny pads, one on the back of his tongue and one on his palate. Inevitably a certain amount of rubbish, leaves, bark and the like stick to his tongue when he's feeding and these are discarded in his cylindrical droppings.

Echidnas are found all over Australia, their only requirement being a ready supply of ants. They have no established nesting sites and find shelter under logs, bushes, piles of debris or in burrows, Monotremes are unable to maintain a constant body temperature as efficiently as mammals can, and must vary their activities to suit the climate. They avoid extremes of temperature, feeding mainly at night in summer, but in cold weather they are often most active in the daytime.

A mature echidna can weigh up to 7 kg and his spines are a formidable defence against any predator ambitious enough to consider him edible. There are, in fact, few creatures that care to tackle him other than the occasional dingo or, in the case of baby echidnas, a raptor or a large lizard, and since he is non-territorial and solitary he has no reason to be aggressive. When threatened in the open he rolls himself into a tight ball, spines at the ready, or if near a crevice or a hollow log he wedges himself so tightly into it that he is almost impossible to dislodge. On soft earth he has the ability to dig so that he sinks horizontally, disappearing like a lift into its well, and in each case his soft underbelly is protected by his helmet of spines. Many of Tehree's injured echidnas are brought to her because someone has tried to dig them out of the ground, not realising that when he does his lift-well trick the echidna spreads his legs out on either side of his body to hold himself firmly in place. The spade that slices into the earth too close to him may shear off one or more legs or even his beak, and when his beak or his tongue is badly damaged he is under sentence of death.

One should never underestimate an echidna. They may look slow, top-heavy and serious going about their normal business, but they are capable of surprising agility, besides being expert climbers. There was an occasion when one of the baby Jirrahlinga echidnas got out of its pen and had to be detached, with difficulty, from the top of an eight foot chain wire fence. They have a serious dislike of confinement, plus the talents of Houdini when it comes to escape. Tehree explains what can happen.

'A policeman I knew, a man of very orderly habits, phoned me to say he had an echidna in his garage. He'd put it in a box but would I please come and fetch it and release it in a suitable place?

'Not in a box!' I said, knowing echidnas. 'It'll be out of that in two minutes.'

'Don't worry,' said the cop. 'It won't get out of the box and if it did it can't hurt anything.'

'In due course I turned up at the policeman's house and he took me to his garage. We opened the door, turned on the light and were both speechless. The echidna had not only got out of the box but he'd managed to get up on a bench which held a collection of tins of coloured paints. They'd been in recent use, their lids were not on properly and the echidna had bowled them round the garage decorating everything in sight. The floor, the walls and even the policeman's immaculate silver motor car dripped paint in rainbow colours. The echidna was marching through the mess with wet yellow feet and a blue beak.

An Echidna

'I admired the policeman. He just sighed and said, "Well, It could be worse, at least it's water-based paint." '

Tehree's tip, should you ever have to transport an echidna from one place to another, is to use a dustbin. This has no claw-holds for climbing and the echidna is easily removed when you reach your destination.

I was curious to know how Tehree set about rearing baby echidnas because it seemed to me that feeding would be a problem. For one thing their beak is not designed for bottle feeding and for another their milk in the mother's pouch comes from ducts on her abdomen, an ooze rather than a nipple-directed supply.

'You've seen those old-fashioned rice cookers?' Tehree said. 'They're a bit like two round wire sieves, hinged so that they open out. You wrap up the baby echidna to keep it warm and put it in the bottom half, then tape a sea sponge filled with its formula into the top half and close it up. The baby lies on its back as it would do if it was feeding in its mother's skin fold and presses against the sea sponge with its beak to get the milk.. It's pretty much like its mother's pouch would be, and they soon learn to press against the sponge to squeeze more formula through.

'Later on they get to more advanced food so we've got imitation anthills too. There are times when you have to know just how much nourishment a baby's taking and you can put the food inside the anthill with a hole for the baby to feed through, then measure how much it's taking. When they get to the anthill stage their feeding's more complicated. You can't very well keep up a supply of ants and anyway not every variety of ant is suitable. You have mix up a kind of creamy, semi-solid mess of ingredients and supplements as a substitute. We make the anthills here at Jirrahlinga using a plant pot for a mould and polythene piping to form the feeding holes.'

In view of the time that a young wild echidna spends with its mother after it leaves the pouch, about nine months of concentrated learning-by-example, one would have to wonder how well a young hand-raised animal would do when released. However devoted the human carer may be it's clearly impossible to duplicate the mother's pursuit and consumption of ants by means of the tongue, nor can you teach it exactly where to find ants. Reaction to danger, horizontal descent into soft ground, suitable shelter and all the rest of the things an echidna needs to know are largely instinctive, but in the wild the baby has seen them all performed by its mother and has copied them. Tehree says that most juvenile echidnas, including the hand-raised ones, go through a unique and mysterious period known as torpor from which they wake as bush-wise, capable adults.

'It has no relationship to seasonal hibernation as in bears,' she says, 'but both young and adult echidnas go into torpor. Their body temperature drops and they become rigid so that they seem to be dead. I've nearly put a torpid echidna into a body bag myself because I thought it was dead. It usually happens towards the end of winter and it can last for three to six weeks. Baby echidnas are fascinating when you're raising them, affectionate and funny and they go into a complete frenzy over their food. Then they'll go into torpor and when they come out of it they don't want to know you, they're suddenly grown up and ready to be echidnas. It's a mystery how it happens. If you have a young one that doesn't go into torpor you have to put it with other echidnas so that it can learn everything from them.'

The Platypus
Ornithorhynchus anatinus

Considering how different the platypus is from the echidna one would hardly suspect their relationship at first glance. These two are the only surviving monotremes, classified as mammals but possessing characteristics that set them apart. We can relate quite easily to the echidna. After all, he's not unlike an English hedgehog, although he's a totally different species. But nothing else in all the world looks like a platypus.

Consider his outward appearance, a mixture of duck, otter and Walt Disney fantasy; duck's bill, webbed feet and smooth, outer coat of guard hair above a dense, impervious fur that stays dry for hours in the water. Both the platypus and the echidna lay eggs, soft, reptilian eggs instead of giving birth to placental babies like other mammals. Like the echidna, platypus are unable to retain constant body warmth as effectively as other mammals, so they must alter their behaviour and activities to retain a suitable temperature and avoid excessive heat or cold. Lastly their brain has less learning capacity than that of other mammals. Scientists believe that their lack of adaptability, mentally and otherwise, may be the reason why so few monotremes have survived the evolutionary process.

All this makes the platypus a very exclusive and valuable Australian citizen, albeit a shy one who shuns human contact. An encounter with a platypus on our lakes or waterways has a magical quality about it, but only if you keep very still will you see it for more than a few seconds before it disappears. If you are a fly-fisherman, moving slowly through the water, you may see something almost, but not quite, like a large, rising trout. You may even cast a fly towards it, thinking it's a trout. Then, when you realise what it is and if you stand motionless, a platypus may swim close to your legs, mistaking you for a dead tree.

The platypus builds an oval burrow in the bank, just above the waterline and protected by roots or branches. Mating takes place in the water and the pregnant female then digs herself a nesting burrow, longer and more complex than the other, ending in a terminal chamber lined with damp herbage. About two weeks after mating she produces two soft eggs, usually stuck together side by side, and incubates them by holding them against her belly with her tail. The eggs hatch in another one to two weeks and the babies feed on milk secreted in ducts on the mother's abdomen, as does the echidna's baby, for four to five months. During this long nursing period the mother leaves her babies and goes off to find food but there is no parental interaction by the male. The platypus is an essentially solitary creature; mating requires contact, but friendly burrow cohabitation is definitely something else. On the other hand the sharing of an area of water, sometimes by quite a large number of platypus, is permissible.

The baby platypus is naked when it hatches and takes about six weeks to open its eyes and start to grow its coat. At this young stage it has milk teeth on the inside of its bill, but these fall out as it gets older and as an adult it grinds its food between its tongue and hard, horny plates on the upper and lower jaws. Its food consists mainly of invertebrates, worms and freshwater shrimps sifted through its soft bill from the mud or gravel on the bottom of the waterway. It stores the food in pouches in its cheeks under water, rather in the manner of a hamster, and surfaces to eat it on dry land. Its bill is the essential tool on which the platypus is utterly reliant because its eye, ear and nostril apertures close under water. The bill has touch receptors in the skin that enable the animal to find its food and to navigate, and a platypus with a badly damaged bill is as helpless as an echidna with a crushed beak.

Surprisingly perhaps, the platypus has a voice which has been described variously as a growl, a squeak and a whistle or a combination of all three. Very few people get close enough to these creatures to hear their voice and even Tehree, who has heard it in her role of carer, finds it hard to describe. She has had six platypus brought to her at Jirrahlinga, and knowing the animal's notorious susceptibility to stress she was very nervous of handling the first one. It was a female that had been injured in a rabbit trap and picked up near Winchelsea.

'I took her to my vet and said perhaps I should take her straight to the Zoo, because I hadn't had any experience with a platypus. He said, "Rubbish, just take her home and look after her, she'll do fine.

I'll see her again tomorrow." This was before there was the present network of people you could ring for advice and information and she obviously had to have a hide of some sort to live in, water to swim in and suitable food. I got on to one of the keepers at the Zoo about the food and he told me that worms, yabbies and shrimps would keep her going. "Great," I thought. "And where do I get them?"

'I decided to put a story in the local paper about the dangers of rabbit traps near river banks where wildlife go to drink, and also about our platypus and the need for a supply of food for her. The response was amazing, the replies alone took more time than enough but the food came in and the platypus ate everything we offered it. I'd like to think that she loved me for myself alone but I suspect she got to know me because I fed her, she'd nuzzle my hand when I brought the food, making funny little noises. She was a delight, but I didn't want her to get too people-friendly.

'She recovered from her injury very quickly but on the tenth day after she arrived she seemed very restless, moving round her pen as if she wanted to get out. I let her into the grassed area outside the pen and she made straight for the boundary fence as if she wanted to get through. I put her back in the pen and she was really agitated, wanting to get out again and when I let her out she went straight back to the same spot on the boundary. I rang the vet and asked him to come over and see what she was doing because I was worried. I said, "When I let her out she heads for the fence in a direct line to where she came from, I think she wants to go home." Every time I left her that day she made a funny kind of whistling sound as if she was trying to tell me something, and I felt very depressed.

'The vet finally arrived after dark. He didn't seem too worried, said she was fine but to keep her for another day or two, and left. She was getting more and more frantic so a while later I rang him and said, "With all due respect, I'm taking her back now." He thought this was crazy in the middle of the night, but I called a friend to come with me and we drove the platypus back to the place where she'd been found, near a river. We released her a few metres from the water and she made straight for it; I thought for a moment she was going to leave without even a goodbye but right at the water's edge she stopped and turned back towards us. She looked at us for a minute and made a funny whistling sound, then dived in and was gone, but I knew she had said goodbye, and thank you.'

Platypus can travel quite long distances over land but because the web on their front feet extends beyond the end of their toes they fold the toes under and walk on their knuckles. In the water they use their front feet for swimming and their back feet are tucked under their tail and used only for steering or as brakes. The male has sharp, hollow spurs on his hind legs linked to poison glands, and these can cause excruciating pain to anyone who picks him up carelessly. The female has only rudimentary spurs in her youth and loses them as an adult. Apart from the male's spurs they have no defence against predators other than their aquatic lifestyle. Dogs, feral cats, goannas or eagles would all eat them if they could catch them, but now their greatest danger comes from human abuse of their habitat. Our development of riverbanks and canals, the setting of traps near water, abandoned fishing lines and nets and pollution in the water all threaten their survival.

Tehree has now developed effective temporary housing for distressed platypus at Jirrahlinga. She describes it like this. 'We lay about two metres of large plastic piping leading down to a small drum about two-thirds of a metre underground and line both the drum and pipe with leaves and earth. We put a bath or a plastic swimming pool in the ground near the burrow entrance, fill it with water and put an astro turf mat in the bottom of the pool, then feed the platypus in the pool.

'The thing everyone should remember about platypus is that they're so easily stressed, and stress can kill them quicker than anything else. They're very delicate mentally and they need expert care. If you ever come across a platypus that needs help wrap it in a towel to keep it warm, at a constant temperature, and get it to the nearest vet or the Zoo as soon as you can. And be sure you remember that the male platypus has spurs.'

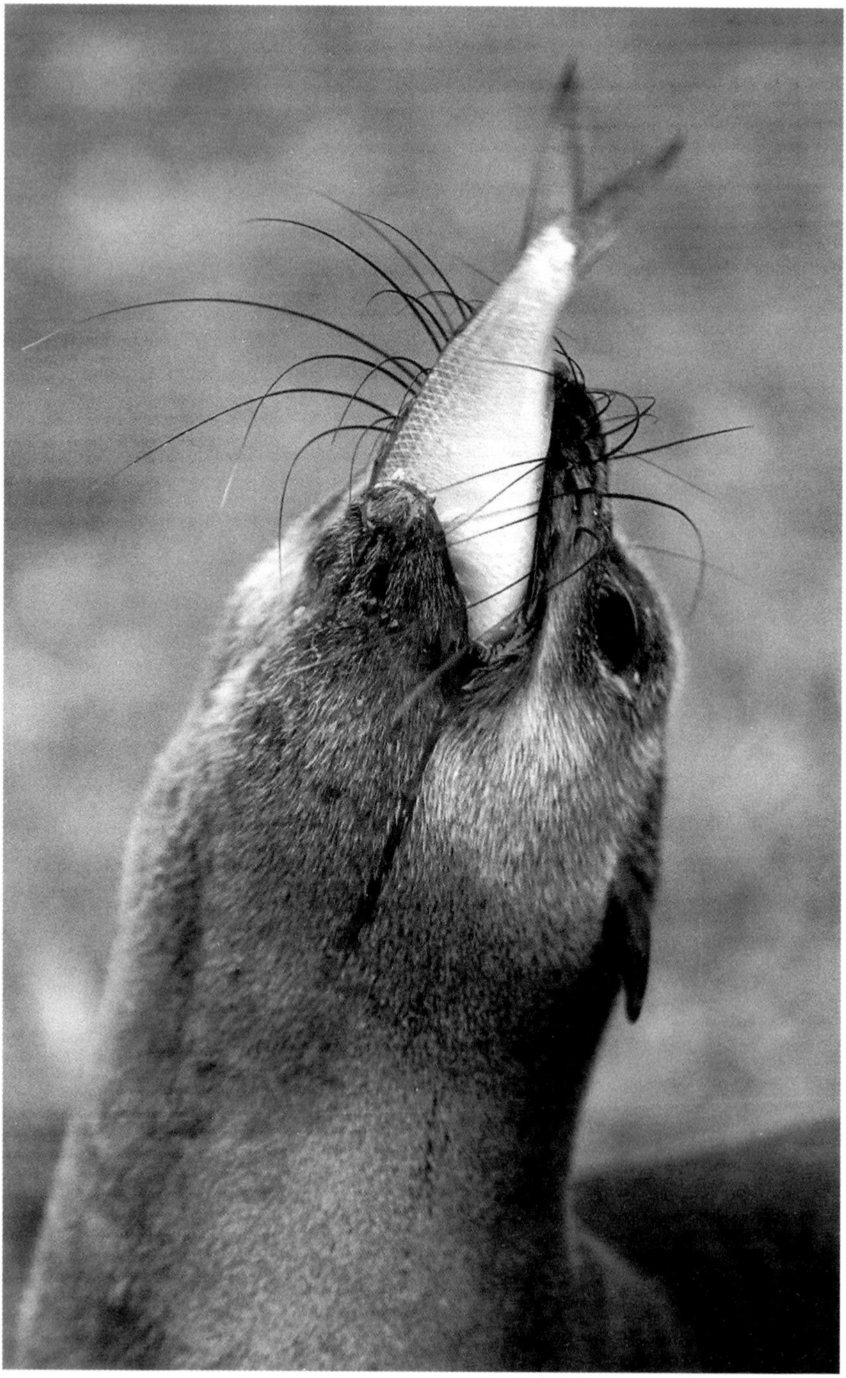

9   Seals and Dolphins

ALMOST EVERY Wildlife Shelter in the State deals routinely with birds, lizards and even the occasional snake, and Shelter operators become blasé about kangaroos, possums, wombats, and, if they're common in the Shelter's area, koalas. Jirrahlinga, being on the south coast, also deals with seals, as well as other aquatic mammals and seabirds. Seals in particular require a quite separate and unique expertise, a closed book to those who run Shelters far removed from the coastal areas.

In the course of Tehree's business she's routinely called out to collect or to help any species of animal, bird or reptile that exists in the Victorian countryside, or in its coastal waters. The aquatic creatures may be injured, sick, orphaned or a combination of all three, and they require great expertise in capture, handling and transport, not to mention subsequent treatment. This expertise can only come from experience because there are no text books on the subject, but Tehree, having coped single-handed with rescues for years, has reduced them to an art form. In the case of seals, wild animals with formidable bite-power and a natural aversion to humans, Tehree's capture technique is simple and efficient, as we will shortly see, but she'd be the first to point out that when you've caught your seal the fun is only just beginning. You then have to deal with a variety of seal-related problems to which there is no easy answer.

In the beginning Tehree was fairly ambivalent about seals, particularly as patients at Jirrahlinga. She'd already had one seal episode when she was working as the Bellarine Peninsular Shire Ranger. On that occasion she was quite relaxed when she was asked to go and collect a baby seal from a beach, one holiday weekend in summer.

'There's a lot of visitors down there,' she'd been told, 'and people are teasing the poor thing. Put it in your utility and take it back to your place.' This'll be interesting, she thought, and a baby won't be too difficult to handle. It sounded quite a simple job. Tehree loaded some rope into the back of her Shire Ranger's utility, her large German Shepherd into the front and picked up a friend of hers who'd enjoy the drive. When they reached the beach it was indeed packed and a large part of the crowd was standing in a circle, all gazing at something in the centre. Tehree, unable to see through the crowd, climbed onto the back of the utility and peered over their heads.

'I had been told it was a baby seal, but what I saw was a half-grown elephant seal, a bull, and they weigh about half a ton. There was no way I could possibly move it but something had to be done. Apart from the people who were just staring there was a mob of young drunks, and they were the ones who were tormenting it. While I was watching it bellowed at them, and one of them threw a cigarette butt into its mouth while the others chucked beer cans at it.'

'I didn't know quite what to do but I got the ropes out of the back of the utility, and some stakes, and my friend and I staked the ropes in a circle round the back of the crowd. Then I turned on the flashing light on top of the ute and blew the horn. They all turned and looked and I shouted, "Everyone outside the ropes, please.'

'Most of them went outside the ropes, all except the drunks who turned nasty. Two of them had knives and they were poking the poor thing, stirring it up. It bit one of them and he had to go to hospital which was good, but the one who'd thrown the butt into its mouth came weaving over to me, waving his arms about and muttering.

'"Who d'you think you are?" he said. He was so drunk he was slobbering and he used a lot of foul language. I wasn't feeling too secure, I only weighed about eight stone and I was standing on the running board to get a bit of extra height, but just then my German Shepherd put his head out of the car window, looked at this guy and yawned. Then he climbed out of the car and lay down in front of me.'

'The drunks took one look at the dog and backed off. I knew I was on a winner then so I shouted, "Out! Get out behind the ropes," and they did.

'After that the only problem was the seal. He was sick and we couldn't move him back into the water, so for three weeks, twenty-four hours a day until he got better, we had to look after him. Friends of mine and other volunteers helped and between us we took care of him. Sam, we called him in the end. I did the night duty in the ute every night, with two German Shepherds and a poodle to keep me company.

'When I got down there one night I found that men from the Department of Natural Resources & Environment had got there first and were trying to force Sam back into the sea. They had a strange way of doing it, they poured petrol on the water and set it on fire and then fired shots into the air to frighten him. I was so furious I set the dogs on them. For one thing Sam couldn't go back to the sea then. He was sick with something we never identified, but also he was moulting so he might have drowned or got hypothermia. When they're moulting their coat leaks and they have to stay on land.

'I got Mr Bob Warnecke, the seal expert with the DNRE, to come down and he confirmed that Sam had come to the beach to moult. He thought he might be the same elephant seal that'd been seen in the Maribyrnong River two or three years earlier, and I persuaded

Before the swimming pool was built seals had to make do with the bath.

him to come down to the beach and tag Sam before he went back to the sea. Two years later Sam came up on the beach near Geelong to moult and was identified by his tag, then two years after that he appeared at Warrnambool with two cows.'

'My little poodle formed an amazing bond with Sam. She wouldn't let anyone go near him but she herself would go close up to him and kind of talk to him, little soft barks and whimpers and you could see he liked her. Elephant seals don't move well on land, they have the wrong hind flippers and they're immensely heavy, but the police rang me one night to say that there was an enormous animal halfway up one of the streets leading from the beach. It was making a terrible noise and should they shoot it.

'I said "No! Don't you dare shoot him, I'm coming right away!" and the poodle and I rushed off in the car. The police had closed off the street and there was our huge Sam, very upset, bellowing about it all and the police frantically keeping people back. Heaven knows what Sam thought he was doing there. Anyway, the poodle went up and talked to him and he recognised me so he humped himself round and we walked him back to the beach, me on one side and the poodle on the other. The police were amazed.'

When Tehree is called upon to retrieve a normal-sized seal from a beach there's the matter of transport, not to mention safe confinement during transport. To drive a car with a disturbed seal loose in the back would be foolhardy in the extreme so Jirrahlinga has developed folding wire cages, easily stowed and erected when needed for rescues.

Tehree was called one day to collect no less than three seals, all stranded at different points along the coast. It was a fine, warm day and out of the kindness of her heart she invited an elderly female friend to come with her for a quiet drive. She loaded three collapsible cages into the back of the station wagon and they drove off. A short time later she had a call from Jirrahlinga on her mobile phone. 'There's another seal, a baby on the beach with a dead mother,' they said. 'It's a bit further down the coast so could you please pick it up when you've got the others?'

'I've only got three cages,' Tehree said. 'I haven't anywhere to put it.'

'Well, it's got to be picked up. You'll have to manage somehow.'

She collected the first three seals without incident, caged them in the three cages and then scratched her head, wondering where she could put the fourth seal. Her passenger, though enjoying the weather and the view, was showing signs of serious unease at the presence in the car of three marine wild animals, even though they appeared to be restrained.

'The next one's only a baby,' Tehree told herself, moving the occupied cages so that they formed a triangle. 'It can go in the middle here, on the floor.'

She picked it up some distance further on and placed it in the space between the cages, turned the car and headed for home. All seemed peaceful except for her visibly nervous friend, but when she glanced in the rear vision mirror she saw that the baby seal had climbed on top of the cages and was about to join them in the front seat. In view of her passenger's age and sensitivity to seals this seemed undesirable.

'NO!' yelled Tehree, braking sharply and pulling in to the side of the road. Then she thought, 'That's no use, what does "No" mean to a baby seal. I've got to do seal talk.' She swung herself round and barked loudly at which the seal, recognising the language of it own kind, backed obediently into its hole between the cages. Seals are skilled climbers; Tehree drove on but the baby, sociable and inquisitive, persisted in its efforts to join them while Tehree, only too aware of her passenger's increasing panic, barked herself hoarse, uttered useless reassurances and tried to keep her eyes on the road.

When it was all over, the seals unloaded and the elderly lady's heart rate restored to a normal level Tehree drove her home. 'Thank you dear,' she said as she got out of the car. 'But I thought you asked me to come for a nice, *quiet* drive.'

Ordinary seals are a more manageable size than Sam, but anyone who has looked inside a seal's mouth will have a profound respect for their teeth. A fish diet requires much the same dental equipment as a flesh diet so seals have developed jaws to rival the jaws of a dog, and they have no inhibitions about using them on people. This small personality flaw is contrary to their looks which might have been designed by Walt Disney. They have eyes and lashes fit for a prima ballerina and the grace, underwater, to match. They have lovelier curves than Mae West, flippers they use can use almost like hands, their own language and wonderful whiskers, stiff, sensitive, movable whiskers that express their moods. It's a mystery why Disney chose to immortalise a mouse rather than a seal. Mice, after all, have somewhat dull personalities and the most unattractive habits.

Tehree says that until she really got to know seals she regarded them with respect as animals which could survive in the perilous environment of the ocean, but that she never suspected them of being distinct, responsive individuals. When she began to raise orphaned and injured seals at Jirrahlinga she changed her mind and became fascinated by them. At the present time she has three young seals, Flipper, the eldest, and two babies.

Flipper arrived in a bad way, sick, dehydrated and utterly opposed to accepting the nourishment necessary for his survival. When he finally decided to sample a little food his taste was for quality rather then quantity, and while Flipper ate expensive salmon Hamish and Tehree, whose budget as usual was limited, made do with cheap fish. Flipper, and any other young resident seal, has the use of the family swimming pool and the run of the garden. In Flipper's case the TV set has been installed near the swimming pool, right beside the house, so he has night time entertainment to keep him quiet. If for some reason the picture cuts out Flipper barks and complains until someone wakes up and comes to fix it.

Tehree declares with pride that no creature at Jirrahlinga is spoiled and I'd be the last to dare point my finger at Flipper, but if a young seal has to have a temporary substitute for aquatic life this one has landed in a very cushy situation. His devotion to Tehree is touching. The seal follows her round, comes at her call, goes in the car with Tehree to the beach for a proper ocean swim and behaves like a spoiled child when Tehree, having taken him down to the larger swimming pool in the Sanctuary-proper, goes out of his sight.

'I was swimming him down there the other day,' Tehree told me. 'I'd swum the two baby seals already. They get jealous if I swim them all together so I swim them one at a time. I was sitting on the side of the pool, reading a book while Flipper had his turn and he'd come up every few minutes and give me a nudge on my right side, then go off and play in the water again. Suddenly he came charging up on my left side and that isn't so good since I had a stroke. He gave me such a push that I toppled over into the water, clothes and book and all.'

'I was furious and it was cold too, but Flipper thought it was terrific and got very excited. He belted round the pool, turning somersaults and diving and barking until I saw the funny side of it and started to laugh. As soon as he saw me laughing his behaviour changed, he swam up to me and round me clapping his flippers and making funny little glad sounds, as if to say "Good, you're laughing, isn't this fun!" When I tried to climb out of the pool he barked and nudged at me to stop me, so I realised that this was a really good seal game and he didn't want it to end.'

The rescue of injured seals when they're adult, sick or hurt and understandably hostile, is not an activity for the inexpert handler. Seals aren't built for manhandling because they are smooth as marble, very strong and built in a continuous series of curves. If trying to grab a grown wombat can be likened to catching a greased pig, seals are worse, and also they have a formidable bite. They can, however, be persuaded to move in a forward direction and on this simple principle Tehree has based her seal-catching technique. Her equipment seems unlikely at first glance, no ropes, no cages, no dart guns but only an seal-sized net with a long handle like butterfly net, and a sack. The seal's attention being engaged from the front Tehree approaches it from behind, puts the butterfly net with the sack inside it over the seal's head and urges it forward, so that the sack covers its front end and can be pulled down its body as it moves. The whole operation takes a matter of seconds, the end of the sack is tied and a neatly packaged seal is ready for transport.

She tells of being called to pick up a seal one day by the Conservation Department and arriving on the beach to find a Department officer, complete with smart sunglasses, mobile phone and helper, eyeing the seal from a safe distance.

Flipper emerges cautiously from the seal swimming pool at Jirrahlinga.

'"What are you here for?" he asked me.

'I said, "I'm here to pick up that seal, the Department called me."

'"How are you going to do that?" says the Ranger. He was looking at the butterfly net and the sack and sneering. "You can't catch seals with a butterfly net."

'"Well, how are you going to do it?" I said to him, "With your mobile and your sunglasses?" I marched down the beach and two minutes later the seal's in the sack. The man didn't know what to say but he helped me carry the seal back to the car.

'You very often have an audience on the beaches when you have to capture a seal and they get very excited about it. There was another time I was called to collect a seal and the beach was crowded, the people all standing round looking at it. It was a big seal and pretty stirred up. I had a friend with me and I got her to go round in front of it to get its attention but before she even got there I'd slipped the net over its head and had it in the bag. If you miss the first chance with them it's much more of a battle and this one was getting very cranky inside the bag anyway. We had to carry him up the beach between us to the car and halfway up a woman came running after us with a camera.

'"Oh, that was wonderful!" she said. "It was so quick! I didn't even have time to get a photo. Look, do you think you could possibly let him go and do it again so that I can get a good snapshot?"

'I was hot and the seal was heavy, as well as carrying on like a caged tiger in the sack. The only way I'd have let it out again was if I'd been sure it would bite her and not me.'

Tehree is adamant that no-one, however kind hearted, should collect a baby seal, apparently abandoned on the beach, and take it home. 'Female seals always give birth on land,' she says, 'and then go off into the sea to feed. A baby seal may be left alone on the beach for several days while the mother's off foraging, but she always knows when to come back.

'You'll be making trouble both for the seals and yourself if you take a baby away because young seals are very expensive to feed, and difficult too. They need quantity, quality and variety as well in their fish diet, and they'll quite likely refuse to take anything at all at first, in which case you'll have to force-feed them or possibly stomach tube them if they're very young. Don't try it. The immediate instinct of any rescued seal, even young ones, is to bite their rescuer and believe me, they can bite. When you have to feed them by forcing fish down their throat one person has to hold their mouth open while another one pushes in the fish, and the one doing that needs to have great faith in the holder because otherwise they can lose a finger.'

'Seals become humanised very quickly. This can mean that they're unsuitable for release and they have to be kept in captivity for life, which may be twenty years. Most people have no facilities, either for preparing a seal for release or for keeping them in captivity long-term so don't even consider it; call an expert and leave it to them to help the animal.

'Seals spend quite a lot of time on land, apart from when they're giving birth. They may be moulting, when their coat leaks and they can't stay in the water for long. They may come ashore to rest or sunbathe, and they look on the beach as their rightful place as much as they do the sea so leave them alone, unless they're obviously hurt or ill. If you can see something's really wrong with them ring the local police or the Zoo. They'll send someone who can assess whether they need help or not, but don't try to handle them yourselves. They're lovely creatures so just enjoy watching them.'

Another trap for the seal rescuer is their ability to escape from the average garden or enclosure, however well fenced, and once out they can travel for long distances over land. Tehree had a telephone call at 1 am from a man who had found a young seal in a carpark and taken it home. It seemed very friendly, he said, but he felt that a carpark was the wrong place for it and it might get hurt. He'd intended to phone Jirrahlinga about it in the morning, but he'd just been out to his dog-proofed garden to check on it and it had disappeared. Tehree got into her car and started to search, but at quarter to three she heard that the seal had been located, by a policeman who'd been called to investigate an intruder at a pensioner's home. The dog-proof fencing had been a breeze to climb and the seal had travelled approximately 5 kilometres. On another occasion a pilot reported that he couldn't land on the Barwon Heads airfield because there was seal in the middle of the runway. This one wasn't an escapee but a wild seal which had apparently swum up the Barwon River and decided to take an overland route back to the sea.

Then there was the time the local police rang Jirrahlinga to say that there was a seal at the roundabout outside the Barwon Heads Hotel. Would someone please come and collect it immediately, as it was holding up the traffic and menacing the policeman in attendance by running towards his legs and making a funny kind of sobbing noise.

When Tehree and Catherine, one of her staff, arrived at the roundabout Tehree's heart plummeted. 'Catherine,' she said, 'Do you see what I see? It's ours!' The last time she'd seen the young seal was in the Sanctuary swimming pool behind an eight foot cyclone fence. The policeman seemed seriously upset by his brush with a wild animal and Tehree decided it would be unwise to admit ownership, particularly as she had no idea at all how it had got out of its enclosure. She whispered to Catherine, 'Pretend it's a wild seal and let's get it home.'

It recognised Catherine, its keeper, as soon as it saw her and charged towards her making joyful noises. Tehree, straightfaced, shouted, 'Watch it, Catherine! Don't let it get you!' They capered round in front of it as though terrified while the poor seal, longing only for comfort, no doubt believed they'd gone mad. Catherine finally did a mock rugby tackle, wrapped it in a blanket and leapt into the car to give it a good cuddle. It was kinder not to tell the policeman that its advance on his legs and the 'sobbing noise' had only been asking for help and sympathy. He'd have a better story to tell his mates if he believed he'd been threatened by a monster.

When Tehree and Catherine arrived back at Jirrahlinga they put the seal back in the pool enclosure and retreated to a place where they could watch it without being seen. The seal, happy to be home, swam, played and slept, then decided to repeat his recent escape. He went to the corner of the eight foot chain wire fence and using both his front and back flippers went up and over it with the skill of a cat.

Seals, like everything else, are subject to injury, illness and death in the wild, but far too often Jirrahlinga's orphans and the injured seals are the victims of human behaviour. Nets, fishing lines that wrap around their necks and choke them and bullets, fired by fishermen who look on them as competition or just by gun-happy idiots, account for a great many seals. Tehree marks the seals that come to her by clipping a square on their head before they are released into the sea, and she tells of the misery of finding the corpse of a seal, Jirrahlinga-raised and marked, washed up on the beach full of bullet holes. One can understand the commercial fisherman and perhaps excuse him for shooting seals, if he genuinely believes that they threaten his livelihood; at least he's likely to shoot them cleanly and sparingly. It's impossible to comprehend the twisted minds of the people who shoot these creatures for no reason at all, often leaving them to bleed to death or be torn apart by sharks,

Humans can be so incomprehensibly cruel. There was a recent case of a young seal at Sorrento. It came up near a fishing boat and the occupant threw it fish which it ate enthusiastically. Later it surfaced near the pier and more fish were donated. The seal must have decided that it had struck gold and that humans were harmless, benevolent food dispensers, created solely for the benefit of seals. Then, one day, a woman looking through binoculars from the cliff saw it circling a fishing boat and the fisherman throwing fish to it. This time the fish were attached to lines, the hooks still in their mouths. The seal came up on the beach to die and the post mortem disclosed an intestine full of nylon line and hooks.

This mindless sadism is a threat to all our wildlife, as well as black shame on the people responsible for it. To kill for food is acceptable and to cull, when it's done professionally, is often done in the animal's best interest, to prevent over-population and starvation. To kill for the pleasure of killing is an obscenity. Spotlighters blaze away at night and then go home for a booze-up leaving dead and injured animals in the bush, drivers swerve dangerously to run over snakes on the road and feel heroic. Every duck shooting season sees heavy mortality among rare birds that could not possibly be mistaken for ducks, but have committed the crime of flying within range of the shooters. All this is so pointlessly cruel that one sometimes wishes one could apply the rule of 'an eye for an eye' in its most literal sense. No doubt the courageous marksman who shoots a seal, which presents him with an almost foolproof target, cuts another notch on the stock of his gun and feels like John Wayne, triumphant at the end of a B Class Western.

There's a happier side to the story of seals who fall foul of the human race. Thanks to Tehree, I had the privilege of seeing one of her young seals, fat, healthy and aggressive, released back into Port Phillip Bay. He'd come to Jirrahlinga a few months earlier, very sick and with a broken rib. The rib injury was a legacy of his first contact with humans. Illness had forced him up on a beach where he lay in deep distress, until two of our more sensitive citizens happened to come across him in the sand.

'It's dead,' said one of them, giving the little seal a sharp kick.

'No it's not,' said his companion, 'I just saw it move a bit.' He gave the juvenile a heftier kick, thereby breaking its rib. 'Look, it's alive.'

An elderly couple, walking on the beach, retrieved the honour of the human race by objecting, then phoned Jirrahlinga and the little seal, more dead than alive, was taken into care. Tehree said that it should have died. It would eat nothing at first; they fed it by stomach tube and for three nights she slept with it, constantly checking it. Gradually it began to eat, accepting only the choicest fish, and slowly it recovered, but humans other than Tehree were enemies and treated as such.

Like all her seals at Jirrahlinga he was known as Flipper, her dogs being trained not to harass anything called by that name. During his convalescence he was given the run of the garden, the use of the pool in the fernery beside the house and generally treated as an honorary family member. Tehree, however, was determined that he, like all the other seals she rescues, remain a true seal, and that when he was ready to return to aquatic life he would be able to cope. To ensure his future safety it was necessary to create conditions as close as possible to those a seal would meet in the sea. When he was fully recovered his living quarters were changed to the larger pool, ringed by a high cyclone wire fence far down the Sanctuary and his meals became irregular, as they would be when he had to rely on self-caught fish. Pumps were installed at either end of the pool to create mock waves and currents and a canvas barrier raised around the pool's rim, so that he could be forced to spend periods of two hours in the water at a stretch. Contact with humans was kept to a minimum, but from time to time he was placed with adult seals to reaffirm his knowledge of seal behaviour.

Flipper's release was well attended by the media. Jirrahlinga needs publicity to generate the funds to feed baby seals on expensive fish, to say nothing of the food needed for all the other wildlife. Tehree releases many seals without such publicity but this time she notified the Press and they decided it would make a good story, especially with pictures. Flipper regarded the sudden intrusion of strange men bearing inexplicable objects which they pointed at him, with a mixture of confusion and delight, provided they kept their distance. The day before the release there was a session with a television crew who unwisely ventured into the pool enclosure with their cameras, and had to leave in disorder when he charged them. On the day of the release no less than five different media outlets came to wave him goodbye, but they were wise enough to stay outside the fence.

It was an inauspicious day, weatherwise. The morning started cold and cloudy, with the threat of rain. A camera crew set up on the outside of Flipper's fence and Tehree tossed small fish into the pool to make him dive for them. He ate the first one, then planted each successive fish on the bottom for future reference and came up to ask for more. It was clear from the first that he was aware of the camera crew, and increasingly obvious that quite blatantly he was showing off.

Tehree was standing by the fence and he kept coming over to her for approval. Then she hid herself and he gave his full attention to the camera crew, diving to the pool's bottom, retrieving a stored fish, throwing it into the air and catching it, then posing on the pool's edge. He raised his head, stiffened his whiskers and his whole attitude said, 'This is my best profile, are you sure you've got it?' In a Hollywood starlet his behaviour would have been excusable; in a seal on the brink of release it was bizarre. So carried away was he that when Tehree placed the wire catching cage just inside the gate and lured him with yet another fish he waddled in after it, and the first stage of the operation was complete.

Off Queenscliff, close to the Heads of Port Phillip Bay, there are large colonies of seals. This being Spring the majority of younger bulls and cows had transferred to Phillip Island in Westernport Bay, their traditional site for the breeding season, making the introduction of a young stranger such as Flipper to the Port Phillip Bay colony less hazardous. There is always the risk, when you introduce a lone seal to an established colony that he will be resented, attacked and rejected, and then the work that you have done to save him becomes a mere betrayal of his trust. We loaded Flipper onto a motor boat, the Press climbed aboard and we set out for Chinaman's Hat, an old lopsided wooden buoy now occupied by seals. It was on all our minds, especially Tehree's, that Flipper was approaching his moment of truth. Once he was in the sea with strange seals his fate was out of human hands.

The cloud had lifted and the wind dropped. The buoy, as we came alongside, was topped by several old bull seals, elders beyond breeding age who had not bothered to join the move to the breeding grounds. They ignored our arrival, massively rolling to scratch their backs, their eyes drooping lethargically in the emerging sun. These were pompous, short-tempered old gentlemen, superannuated but wise in the ways of the seal world. We rocked gently below them, Tehree wanting them to get Flipper's scent and Flipper theirs. The old bulls knew the boat well enough because Hank, the skipper, specialises in seals and dolphins, taking tourists out to the colonies to watch them and swim with them during the summer. The bulls looked on Hank's boat as a friend, bringing them free entertainment rather than trouble.

Adolescent seals were playing on the lower level of the buoy beneath the stolid bulk of their elders and it was these, Flippers peer group, who would either accept him or reject him, as children will in a schoolyard with a new boy whose face doesn't fit. Animals can be far more cruel than children, lethally cruel, and we were full of anxiety for the little seal.

We motored a couple of hundred metres from the buoy before starting the release. Even the media seemed speechless while his cage was hefted onto the stern of the boat, the gate at its end opened and it was tilted down towards the sea. Flipper regarded his natural element with deep suspicion, turned his back on salt water and scrabbled indignantly back upwards in the cage. Tehree pulled the mat from under him and he slid down the metal floor, over the rim. There was a moment when he clung by his flippers to the cage's edge, his body dangling, eyes wide and whiskers spread, then a splash and he was gone. Everyone was silent, watching the sea and holding their breath.

For a few minutes there was nothing, just small, benign waves, the seal-topped buoy and the sky. Then 'There he is!' and out of the water, curved in ecstatic play, came not one seal's body but two, one with the square Jirrahlinga-shaved head marking: Flipper and his new best friend. Round and round the boat they swam, under it to appear on the far side, sometimes jumping clean out of the water, rolling round each other, diving and reappearing. They both knew we were watching and it was as if they were performing a ballet, an aquatic *pas de deux* to celebrate Flipper's freedom and to show us that all was well. We watched them until they finally vanished together and we knew we'd been shown magic. No-one on that boat could have seen it and not been moved.

One of the pressmen, his voice lowered in awe, said to Tehree, 'If you called him now, would he come to you?'

Tehree eyed him with compassion, for how could he be expected to understand. 'If I called him and he came to me,' she said, 'I'd know that I'd failed him.'

The Australian Fur-Seal

Order *Pinnipedia*, Family *Otariidae*

This is the species of seal that predominates in the waters of southern Victoria and Tasmania, so named because of its fur, a dense under-fur covered by a sleek layer of guard fur, highly efficient insulation against wet and cold. The fact that it was once considered a fashionable covering for the backs of rich women meant that the fur-seal was once most cruelly hunted, almost to the point of extinction. The descriptions of the 19th Century seal massacres round the southern coast of Australia, where thousands of seals were annually bludgeoned to death, are utterly macabre.

Fur seals were once land mammals and they took to the sea more recently than other seal species. They still possess ear-flaps, a relic of the time when they lived on land, and they still move more in the manner of a land animal than other seals, using their hind limbs as well as their front flippers for locomotion. The result may look ungainly but they can move at a surprising speed and, as I've pointed out, are expert climbers. Once in the sea they transform into superb swimmers, capable of diving 130 metres in search of prey, which may include anything from squid and shoaling fish to bottom dwellers such as crabs or crayfish. To deal with this diet the seal has developed the dental equipment of a carnivore, shaking its larger victims until they are broken into a manageable size rather than tearing them apart as a lion, equipped with claws, would do. Indigestible remains such as bones are later neatly vomited.

The female fur-seal is much smaller than the male whose size and strength determine his success in the breeding season. This starts at the beginning of November and ends by the 20th December, a hectic period of birthing and mating and, on the male's part, the protection of territorial rights. Each dominant male maintains his well-defined territory on the traditional breeding sites which may be on rocky headlands, open beaches, islands or rock pools. Females and young seals can move freely between the territories because the males form no personal harems, their aggression towards other males being a defence of their territory rather than of its occupants. On the whole this aggression is vocal and attitudinal rather than physical, although in violent clashes their teeth can inflict serious damage

The traditional breeding sites are both crowded and noisy, close body contact between the females and their young being welcomed rather than avoided. The female has one pup every year, oestrus occurs 3-5 days later and she mates with one of the territorial males after a short courtship. She then goes to the sea to feed and returns to suckle her pup a few days later. She must follow this routine for about 8 months, then introduce her offspring to the sea and teach it to catch and eat its natural food, finally weaning it when it is about 11 months old. The seal reaches puberty when it is 4-5 years old and the male must then develop the size and strength to dominate his own territory before he can breed; until then he may only watch from the sidelines. Not many male seals have a breeding career beyond a few seasons because defeat by younger males, injury, disease, starvation or death by predators always threaten him, and in the end one or other will defeat him.

In the bad old days of the nineteenth century seal slaughters mercifully ended when protective legislation was enacted in 1891. Sealing continued under regulation in Tasmania for another 30 years or so, but now we have at last ceased to commit organised seal slaughter and the Fur-Seal, attractive and resilient, survives in increasing numbers around our shores.

Southern Elephant Seal

Order *Mirounga Leonina* Family *Phocidae*
Sam, the Elephant Seal that Tehree defended on the beach, was a rare visitor to the Australian mainland. His normal range is the Antarctic, breeding on the shores of icy southern islands and spending

long periods at sea. The adult male can grow to 4 metres in length, weigh nearly 4000 kg and has a bulbous, comedian-style proboscis which enables him to produce his great bubbling roar, his main tool for territorial advertisement. The Elephant Seal is designed for swimming rather than for the semi-terrestrial life of the Fur-seal. Their hind legs are useless on land, and in the interest of streamlining the pinna of their ear has disappeared.

The males go ashore to breed in late August, followed by the pregnant females who establish themselves in harems in one or other of the male territories, giving birth to a single pup in September or October. The mother suckles the pup for about three weeks, then abandons it. For seven weeks the pup fasts, playing with other juveniles in the shallows and learning the necessary aquatic skills, then finally takes to the sea when it is about 10 weeks old,

Bones have been found in the ashes of ancient Aboriginal camp sites which establish that the Elephant Seal once colonised the north west coast of Tasmania, and was hunted for food by the Aborigines. Much later, in the 19th Century, on Flinders Island and Macquarie Island where it still bred, it was hunted like the Fur-seal and like the Fur-seal it came very close to extinction. Now, perhaps disillusioned by its contacts with man, it lives mainly where men cannot go.

Dolphins

There are 36 species of dolphins and whales known to inhabit Australian waters but they can not be classed as native Australians. They are citizens of a world where borders and nationalities don't exist and they visit us only when they please. In the case of whales we flock to see them, respect them now although we once slaughtered them, and generally leave them alone. In the case of dolphins, even though we profess to love them we leave nets and lines in their path to trap them. The great mystery is that dolphins still seem to tolerate, even to like the human race.

Tehree has no facilities for dolphins at Jirrahlinga, but since her Rescue Service extends to marine mammals it includes beached and net-entangled dolphins along the southern coast.

'You have to get to them very quickly,' she says. 'They're difficult to help because you can't take a dolphin out of the water as you can a seal. If they're beached they've got to get back in the water straight away or they'll die, and if they're tangled in a net you've got to get in the water with them to cut them loose. You have to keep them afloat and hold them upright in the water. If they are sick or injured you may need expert advice on what's wrong and how best to help them. That's much easier now with email and mobile phones because we can get in touch with a dolphin expert, Wendy Blanchard at 'Sea World'. There was a pod that got beached at Warrnambool and we stabilised them in the water of an inlet there. We checked them for length and sex, took photos of the injuries to their heads and teeth and emailed them to Wendy so that she could tell us what to do for them.

'If dolphins get caught in a net they're panic-stricken and thrash about terribly, hurting themselves, but the strange thing is that if you put your hand on them it's as if they know you're going to help them. They calm down at once and keep quite still. I was telephoned one day by a man who was down here for a holiday, a solicitor, who had seen some dolphins thrashing about near the beach as if they were in trouble. I drove down to the beach and there were two females and a calf caught in a net. Outside the net there were other dolphins, swimming round and round as if they wanted to help them and they were all calling to each other, making a really loud noise.

'I asked the man to go up to my car and phone for help because he was in a beautiful city suit and it didn't occur to me that he'd want to get it wet. He took off his coat though, and came into the water. I told him what to do, to put his hands on the dolphins as I did and they calmed down at once so that I could cut the net and they swam off. The dolphins on the outside clustered round them, examining the baby who was terribly stressed, and then they all disappeared out to sea.

'I turned round and saw that the solicitor had tears streaming down his face and I said, "I'm sorry about your suit," but all he said was. "That was worth a thousand suits."'

'The two females and the baby were seen for some days, swimming up and down quite close in to the shore and it must have been because the mother and her friend were giving the baby dolphin time to recover.'

10 Reptiles

JIRRAHLINGA had no snake exhibit when I first went there, but now it has temperature-controlled snake tanks and Tehree has become an expert, confident snake handler.

Unlike the other animals at Jirrahlinga, many of which are convalescent hospital patients heading for release, the snakes are there for public education, Tehree's passion. Most of Jirrahlinga's specimens are pythons of various kinds, people-friendly creatures that visitors can touch or hold to learn that snakes are really warm and muscular, not cold and repellent as they once believed. The human fear of snakes seems to be in our genes, reinforced by horror stories and parental warnings that condemn all snake-shaped creatures, venomous or otherwise, as innately evil. To touch or hold a snake makes it flesh and blood like ourselves instead of a lurking, half mythical monster.

Although venomous snakes should be treated with the greatest caution and respect there is no reason to consider them evil, for they have been given a defensive weapon and have every right to use it when threatened. In Victoria, where there are no indigenous pythons except in the far north of the state, the chances are that any snake you meet in the countryside will be venomous, to a greater or lesser degree. However, nine hundred and ninety-nine snakes out of a thousand wish only to be left alone, and have a sincere desire to put as much distance between themselves and us as possible.

Early in the season, when they wake from a cold winter, feeling out of sorts as many of us do first thing in the morning, their temper may be rather short. In the breeding season too their hormones may take over and their reactions become unpredictable, but surely we should sympathise with this. Humans have less well-defined breeding seasons, but when they occur our temperaments too become erratic. Snakes are actually beautiful creatures, miraculously designed, without inherent malice towards man and forming a vital link in the natural chain.

When we were living at Kilmore we had a wide, brick verandah along the front of our house and on a hot night when there were bushfires burning, a dull, sinister glow behind the hills, I went out to check whether they were getting closer. As I stood in the dark there was a loud hissing noise, a possum I thought, staring up at the verandah roof to find it. Suddenly I noticed our Siamese cat who had come along the verandah towards me. It was crouched rigid, its tail bottle-brushed, pointing like a bird-dog at something close to me. The noise came again. I looked down to where the cat was staring and beside my bare leg, its head level with my calf and about ten inches away, was a tiger snake. It could have struck at me but instead it had warned me, not once but twice, not to come closer. Tiger snakes do not bite when they stand up, cobra fashion, but it could have had my ankle before I noticed it was there.

I am no hero with tiger snakes. My own estimate of the length of my jump from a standing start would probably not be believed, but I did remember to grab the cat by the tail and take it with me, yowling. The snake vanished discreetly into the dark and the only reason for telling this story is to illustrate my contention that snakes are not perpetually hunting for people to bite. This one, for instance, behaved like a scholar and a gentleman.

There's a small minority group in the world who are Snake People, that is to say people who appreciate snakes, understand them and can handle them without fear on either side. Fear is a curious phenomenon, more readily transmitted between people and animals than between two humans. With people one can be afraid and hide it from them with words and bravado, but human fear is sensed by any animal, however deeply it's hidden. Then the animal is afraid too; it becomes defensive and the trouble starts. There are innumerable stories of small children found playing with snakes unbitten, always because they were too young to feel fear.

Non-venomous snakes, carpet pythons and their like, make the most admirable pets. They neither bark nor growl, need no housetraining and their feeding is simplicity itself compared with nourishment for a dog or a cat; also they need feeding far less frequently. Depending on the snake's size white mice or rats, which can be bought frozen and thawed out, are most acceptable. It's wise, however, not to let your mother-in-law find mice or rats in the refrigerator and get the wrong idea about your dietary preferences. Your pet python will also keep you informed of the warmest place in your house, because that's where he'll be.

Tehree says she was not a natural Snake Person from birth but she has learned to get along with them and to appreciate their virtues. During her time as a Ranger there were inevitable snake incidents when she was called to remove offending serpents from places where they weren't welcome. Realising that it was essential for her to become more familiar with snakes in order to deal with them confidently and efficiently, she considered having one as a pet. A friend of hers was snake-orientated and had several living with her, including a large carpet python named Grimly whom she said would suit Tehree perfectly.

'You'll learn to love snakes if you have Grimly and it's much better to have a big snake, they're easier to find in the house,' she told Tehree. 'The little ones can get into places where you'd never think of looking.'

Tehree, who was still feeling her way with snakes, regarded Grimly with misgiving.

'Why d'you want to get rid of him then, if he's so nice?' she asked.

'Well, my mother-in-law's living with us at the moment, as you know and I keep telling her not to leave her electric blanket on. She got into bed the other night and Grimly had got there first. You couldn't blame him, but you never heard such a fuss. My husband doesn't like him much either.'

To many people the psychological makeup of a true snake fancier may be as puzzling as the mind of someone who dotes on trapdoor spiders and tarantulas, nevertheless such people do exist. Since their more venomous specimens lack the companionable qualities of many other domestic pets, including non-venomous snakes, snake fanciers possess them for both scientific and competitive reasons. Philatelists are very similar: the possession of a rare stamp gives a collector ascendancy over his fellow enthusiasts and they, in turn, must acquire as rare a stamp or be plagued by a sense of inferiority. The equipment required for a stamp collection is fairly simple, but for snake collectors there's the additional complication of licenses, expensive snake accommodation and an assured snake-food supply.

To be a collector of snakes requires time, money and dedication.

It also gets you into some bizarre situations. Tehree tells how she once found herself in the middle of the night in the Ladies' Room of a Caltex service station outside Geelong, transferring some very lively and venomous taipans from a jar into a bag. She was caught in the act by two women, who fortunately mistook them for oversize worms. Why she had to be doing it at that time and in that place is a long and complicated but totally logical story: to a snake enthusiast bizarre situations are the rule rather than the exception.

Victoria lacks the variety of reptile species that inhabit the tropical north, or indeed the deserts of the Centre, but Tiger snakes, Brown snakes, Black snakes and Copperheads flourish in the Victorian countryside. There is abundant food for them, particularly in the wetlands or near rivers, and snakes are now protected by law, an unenforceable conceit since snakes are rarely killed under the noses of people who are going to object, such as DNRE Rangers. The immediate reaction of most Australian men who see a snake is to pound it to death or, if they are in a car, to risk their lives by swerving to run over it. It doesn't seem to occur to them that the death of one isolated snake is futile, unless it is threatening them or theirs. In the case of the car driver there are probably a dozen snakes concealed in the grass just beyond the road, doing no more harm than the one which he has just killed, or more probably maimed. It is very hard to kill a snake with a car unless you brake sharply on top of it; far more likely that you will leave it to die slowly and in agony.

Both the Brown snake and the Tiger snake can be aggressive and both are extremely venomous, the Brown's venom being the more deadly of the two. Luckily the Brown snake's head is small and his fangs set well back in his jaw so that he finds it hard to inject a lethal dose. The Tiger is better equipped and more often the culprit when people get bitten, possibly because he seems to have a fondness for gardens and houses, often sunning himself on doorsteps or even going into a house through an open door. The inevitable uproar when he's discovered frightens him, and he bites in self-defence.

The Black snake and the Copperhead have calmer temperaments

than the Brown or the Tiger, and the Copperhead in particular is a retiring character with a high level of tolerance. The chances are that if you live in an Australian city you'll never see a snake outside the Zoo and even in the country you may rarely see one. Think of them with tolerance rather than fear, don't hunt for them and they won't hunt for you.

Lizards, though they too are reptiles, seldom arouse the same paranoia as snakes and surely this must be because lizards have legs, so we find their method of locomotion more understandable. Birds have wings, fish have fins and all civilised creatures, with the exception of invertebrates such as worms, have two or more legs. We find them all quite acceptable but for some reason we can't handle something which goes about its business on its belly.

The Bluetongue lizard, whose disposition is entirely benevolent, has a head very like a snake's head, and in extreme cases he may be mistaken for a snake. Most Victorians have met a Bluetongue at one time or another, in their gardens or crossing a road, and recognise him for a harmless, pleasant character, but mistakes can happen. Tehree once had a panic call from the local police sergeant, 'Come over here and help me, there's a snake on my doorstep and I can't get out!' She rushed over to find a Blue Tongue lizard sunning himself outside the door and the Sergeant, who fancied himself as a tough, experienced officer, had a hard time living it down.

Bluetongues are good neighbours, and useful to have about the garden since they include snails and other garden pests in their diet and might even be considered decorative, becomingly arranged on a sunny path. They are among the largest members of the Skink family, stout and placid, with malice towards none. As children at Sorrento we had a large dolls-house on our verandah where half-a-dozen Bluetongues lived happily, encouraged by saucers of milk but free to come and go as they pleased. While we sat on the verandah floor talking they sunned themselves comfortably in our laps.

The largest of our Victorian lizards is the Lace Monitor, a relation of the fabled Komodo Dragon and far harder to find than the homely Bluetongue. You could live in Victoria all your life and never see a Lace Monitor, but on a certain part of the Princes Highway near the NSW border you can hardly miss them. It's a wooded stretch where, as you drive towards it, the road seems to be barred with strange, disconnected black shadows. When you are quite close and the shadows hear your car they rise on muscular legs and streak off the road, vanishing into the trees, a startling sight unless you're expecting it. There must be a prosperous and thriving Lace Monitor population in that area; in few other places do you see them actually sunbathing in large numbers on a road.

There are three Lace Monitors at Jirrahlinga at present, the largest and strangest of them being Ralph, strange because he had what must be a unique start in life for one of his species. Lace Monitors would rank very low in the hierarchy of preferred house pets, their normal contact with humans being as good bush tucker. Ralph is an exception, raised in an unusual household that would have affected anyone's personality, and Tehree, who says she'd rather be bitten by a seal than a Lace Monitor, never entirely trusts him.

His previous owner believed in living dangerously, in domestic terms. His household consisted of a girlfriend he'd got pregnant, another girlfriend, also pregnant by him, whom he said should move in with them, and Ralph. The owner's diet featured fish and chips and a constant supply of stubbies, so that was Ralph's diet too. He also slept on the owner's bed. It seems that girlfriend number one, currently sharing the bed and no doubt sorely tried, eventually delivered an ultimatum. It was either her, she told her partner, or Ralph and at that point he capitulated, donating Ralph to Jirrahlinga. There is no record of whether the other expectant mother took his place.

Tehree embarked on her usual routine for weaning animals off alcohol and the wrong diet, gradually teaching Ralph that life was not all beer and fish and chips by cutting down the beer to twice a week, watering it and substituting more appropriate food. Since he'd been used to sleeping in comfort, she allowed him some bedding in the reptile house until he realised that mature Monitors should sleep on the ground but his behaviour, she says, is still not normal Monitor behaviour. When a Monitor is upset or angry he tells you, swelling his throat and hissing, an identifiable warning before attack. Aggro, one of Ralph's companions, is quite explicit about his intentions while Ralph is a silent stalker, malevolent and unreadable even for Tehree, and she is always watchful when she's in his enclosure.

General notes on reptiles

Order: *Squamata*

As Australia has more than 760 species of reptile fauna it would be ridiculous to talk about more of them than the ones I have already mentioned in an anecdotal sense. The State of Victoria lacks the variety of reptile species that occur in the tropics or in the Centre, and while we are by no means reptile-deprived we can't compete with their exotica. In the case of our snakes we hardly see them for half the year because they are torpid during the cold weather, a state which many of us wish we could emulate. However, there are a few facts that apply to them all.

All reptiles are exothermic, relying on an outside source of heat to raise their body temperature to the point where they are capable of activity, and for this reason, in the colder southern winter, they simply sign off. In the tropics or the arid zones finding heat is not a problem. Instead they are preoccupied with finding shade during the heat of the day and in keeping cool enough to maintain their optimum temperature, altering their body posture to reduce heat uptake. At night, in the arid zones where it can become very cold, they take shelter in a burrow or a cave, emerging when the day becomes warm enough to restore their body heat. Reptiles need little water since their bodies have a built-in conservation system, converting soluble body wastes, particularly urea, into solid uric acid. This is a distinct advantage to desert dwellers, whereas aquatic reptiles, such as sea snakes, pass liquid urine.

The skin of a snake or a lizard is inelastic, so as the animal grows it must slough it to make way for the new skin underneath. The snake does this with admirable efficiency, rubbing its nose on a solid object to break the skin, then moving forward so that the whole covering slides off backwards, inside out. Lizards slough piecemeal and are apt to look rather down-market and shabby during the process, stuck about with unshed pieces of the old skin.

Most reptiles lay eggs, depositing them in sheltered places and then apparently forgetting all about them except in the case of pythons and crocodiles, both of which demonstrate some measure of parental conscience. A few species of snake actually carry their young

All reptiles need warmth. A Bearded Dragon under a heat lamp.

inside their body until they hatch, and in other species the embryo develops a placental attachment to the oviduct. Both of these latter cases occur in cool climates rather than the tropics, the internal incubation being protection of the young against the cold. Most newly hatched snakes face the world without parental guidance and with a multitude of predators waiting for them, including members of their own species who regard the rising generation as delicious and quite legitimate food.

Almost all our reptiles are carnivorous, their diet of lizards, smaller snakes, rodents, eggs, frogs and even small birds restricted only by the size of what they can swallow. In the case of snakes the upper and lower jaw can be dislocated to allow them to swallow creatures much larger than their own heads, always swallowing their prey head first to avoid difficulties with the legs. The snake must then retire to a safe place to digest its food, a process that may take a number of days, and a full meal can last it for a considerable time. Snakes can go for weeks without eating, as can crocodiles. Lizards are largely carnivorous but in many cases vary their diet with selected plants, while turtles are mainly herbivorous.

Snakes

Sub-order: *serpentes*
Jirrahlinga provides a home only for non-venomous snakes, but as correct identification of local species is an important part of the service she supplies, I will list the most common ones.

The Eastern Tiger Snake

Notechus scutatus scutatus (Length 120–200 cm)
Like all venomous snakes, the Tiger has hollow fangs in the upper jaw connected to the venom gland by a duct on either side.

The Tiger is one of Victoria's most widely distributed snakes, both venomous and dangerous. He can vary quite considerably in colouring, from tan through to black, with or without the cross-banding which gives him his name. Essentially a shy snake he can become aggressive, flattening his head, inflating his body, rearing up and hissing loudly as a warning. His preferred habitat is supposedly swampy land or near rivers, since frogs are among his favourite foods, but in my experience if a snake is found near or in your house it is likely to be a tiger snake. This may be a consequence of its numbers rather than a taste for human habitation. The Eastern Tiger snake is found in Victoria and eastern NSW as far up as south-eastern Queensland. This subspecies is one that incubates its young internally and in the summer the mother can give birth to as many as 80 young.

The Eastern Brown Snake
Pseudonaja textilis (Length 150–250 cm)
This snake is found in the eastern areas of Australia from southern South Australia through NSW and Queensland into the Northern Territory. It is aggressive and highly venomous, but it is a long, slim snake with a head hardly distinct from its neck. This relatively small head limits its ability to inflict a serious bite but its defence display, body coiled and neck held high in an 'S' bend, it is an impressive sight. It is a diurnal snake, hunting mammals, lizards and frogs and preferring dry areas to wet areas, The female is an egg-layer, producing 10 to 35 eggs.

The Lowland Copperhead
Austrelaps superbus (Length 100–170 cm)
The copperhead lives mainly in southern Victoria and Tasmania, and although its bite is venomous enough to be potentially fatal it is not an aggressive snake, much preferring retreat to confrontation. It may be any colour through reddish brown or grey to almost black and the term 'superbus' must refer to the scales on its side and belly which can be yellow, cream, pink or orange. There are pale bars on the lips and the side of its head and sometimes a dark vertebral stripe down the back. It feeds mainly on frogs and lizards and the female, since the species lives in a cold climate, incubates and gives birth to between 9 and 40 young.

The Inland Taipan
Oxyuranus microlepidotus (Length 150–280 cm)

This is not a Victorian snake, inhabiting western Queensland down through NSW, but I have mentioned it because it was the snake Tehree transferred from a jar to a bag in a service station toilet. In the wild it is placid and shy, but it is credited with being the most poisonous snake in the world and as such has a claim to fame. Few of us would try to disprove its placidity. The Inland taipan is olive-brown to dark brown, the head black and the belly yellow but its scales have a black edge which give it a speckled appearance. It lives in open plains country, feeding on rodents and sheltering in burrows or cracks in the ground, the female laying from 12 to 20 eggs in a clutch. Its relative, the Common taipan, is found from the Kimberleys to the Gulf of Carpentaria and from Cape York Peninsula down the coast to the Queensland-NSW border, and is a far more aggressive snake, very fast-moving, quick to strike and equally feared.

The Australian Carpet Python
Morelai spilota variegata (Length 150–400 cm)

This is but one of the many species of Australian python and the most widely distributed, occurring from the far north of the continent down to the north of Victoria and across the south of South Australia. It is a beautifully marked snake, dark brown fading to red-brown along its sides and with black-edged yellow to cream bands along its body. It feeds on mammals, reptiles and birds and is largely nocturnal although it likes to bask in the sun, often with fellow carpet snakes, during the day. The head is broad-jawed and although it is not venomous it will bite if provoked. The female lays from 9 to 54 eggs between November and January, and like all pythons incubates the clutch by coiling round them until they hatch.

Pythons have heat-sensing pits in the scales of their lips to help them locate warm blooded prey, and 'spurs' on either side of their vent which are the vestigial remains of legs. Some are arboreal, feeding on small birds and arboreal mammals while others, the reptile and rodent eaters, spend most of their time on the ground. All pythons can climb and most will swim. The largest of the Australian pythons is the Amethystine of Cape York which can grow to a length of 850 cm and swallow a wallaby, the smallest the Pygmy python of Western Australia which achieves a mere 60 cm. In between there

An olive python makes an ideal pet.

are a variety of fascinating and beautiful creatures, none of them venomous and some, as I know from experience, capable of forming a close and harmonious relationship with man.

Lizards

Sub-Order: *Sauria*

The Bluetongue Lizard

Tiliqua Scincoides

The Bluetongue lizard belongs to the Skink family, Scincidae, by far the largest and most varied lizard family in Australia. There are 17 lizard families worldwide but only five of them found in Australia, the Geckos, Monitors or Goannas, the Pogopodids, often referred to as legless lizards or sliders, the Dragons and the Skinks. By far the greatest number of these reptiles live outside Victoria, either in the tropical north or in the arid zones, but the Bluetongue can be found over a large area of northern, eastern and southern Australia. He varies from a silvery grey colour with dark bands round the body in the south to a rich brown banded with black in the north. In keeping with his name the tongue is brilliant blue and he can live in almost any habitat, given ground debris or burrows for shelter and insects or vegetable matter for food. The female gives birth to between 5 and 25 young a year and a healthy bluetongue may grow to a length of 55 cm. Like almost all members of the Skink family it has the ability to discard its tail when threatened and to grow a replacement, a trick which distracts its predators and gives it time to escape.

Lace Monitors
Varanus Varius

Australia houses 80% of the world's Monitor species, none of them as large and ferocious as Indonesia's Komodo Dragon, but the Lace Monitor, which is found in Victoria and throughout the whole eastern edge of Australia, is sufficiently impressive. He can grow to a length of 200 cm, living in trees in forested areas but foraging on the ground for small mammals and reptiles, or hunting in the trees for nesting birds and their eggs. He is fond of picnic spots which can yield a delightful supply of discarded food and if disturbed produces a threatening display, distending his throat and hissing loudly. The female Lace Monitor lays her eggs in a termite mound, returning when they ready to hatch to open the nest and release the young.

11   The Birds

WHEN YOU WALK into Jirrahlinga, through the unpretentious wooden gate, past the window where you pay your entrance money, the first thing you're conscious of is birds. There are birds on your right, two cages of them, living together in perfect harmony regardless of the fact that they're a pot-pourri of species, a friendly multi-cultural mix which should be an example to us all. From your left-hand side you will hear the unmistakable voices of Sulphur Crested cockatoos. These are common birds both in terms of number and in the social sense – they all speak the most appalling 'Strine', in captivity and out. I have yet to meet a cockatoo with a posh accent.

Jirrahlinga's mission with birds, as with all other creatures, is to restore them to health after whatever trauma or injury they may have suffered and ultimately to release them. The majority of Tehree's birds come to her because they are damaged in some way and many of these can eventually be cured and set free. Others, often pet cockatoos and parrots, are brought to Jirrahlinga by owners who can no longer keep them, and since these have lived in captivity too long to cope with freedom Tehree, perpetually a soft touch, takes them in.

Tehree's birds come to her with all kinds of injuries, broken wings, broken legs, as fledglings fallen from nests, birds wounded by cats, foxes or shotguns and she is an expert at making them whole. One of the problems in dealing with the variety of birds at Jirrahlinga is their feeding, for there are seed eaters, insect eaters, nectar feeders and birds who require worms and grubs. Sick penguins and other seabirds arrive, needing fish and supplements. The raptors want meat, preferably red and bloody, the fur or feathers still attached while other birds, such as magpies, can only digest non-fibrous meat. Somehow she copes with this dietary nightmare alongside the equally complex requirements of marsupials, reptiles and seals. Almost all wildlife in captivity need supplements with their food because it is impossible to replicate exactly their diet in the wild. Such extras are costly, as are the medications to treat their wounds and illnesses. There is plenty of everything at Jirrahlinga except money but somehow, when it is most needed, Tehree believes that her prime sponsor, God, delivers it. She has has told me of windfall donations and the like when she's been at desperation point and I, for one, can't imagine she could have achieved what she has achieved on her own.

Jirrahlinga's predominant sound is of bird voices. Not of birdsong, because nobody could equate cockatoo voices with song, nor the voices of wild ducks, geese, raptors and rosellas, lorikeets, parrots, or peacocks, all of which are housed in the sanctuary, all talking at once. There are innumerable other birds there as well. The paths winding through Jirrahlinga are flanked by bird cages which many people pass without giving them the attention they deserve, not aware that they are ignoring great treasure. Australian birds are diverse and fascinating, many of them coloured by an artist of genius, others deceptively drab, some large and some tiny, predators and prey, all part of a feathered kaleidoscope, uniquely ours.

The introduced species such as the Sparrow and the Indian Minah are as unwelcome as the cat, the fox and the rabbit and we would be better off without them; they are foreign competition for the rightful owners of our air. The migratory species, terns, swallows and all the rest, may not be Australian nationals but they were coming here long before we arrived, and they have permanent tourist visas. They are as welcome as the seasons that bring them here and they do no harm.

Jirrahlinga houses 82 different species of birds and waterfowl at the present time, and all but 11 of these are native species. In addition there are 10 separate species of ducks and geese, including the enigmatic Cape Barren goose who clearly considers humanity a curious and inferior phenomenon. It will approach you without fear but with the air of a dowager duchess inspecting a chambermaid, eye you from head to foot and turn away with an unmistakable sniff of contempt. There is the Paradise Duck from New Zealand, a large, impressive bird who menaces you with a voice somewhere between a bark and a honk, there are falcons and kites, owls and goshawks. There is a large, lazy Black Cormorant who has been released three times on distant beaches but always returns to sit comfortably on the sand of an enclosure by the gate, awaiting free meals which are served on time.

The Sulphur-crested or White Cockatoo
Cacatua galerita

If I attempted to go into detail about all the bird species at Jirrahlinga, or even all the cockatoo species, this would become an immensely long book, but the Sulphur-crested or White cockatoo is so much part of our lives that he deserves special attention. Apart from Victoria he inhabits the whole north and east of Australia, and is also found in New Guinea, Indonesia, the North Island of New Zealand and a number of other Pacific islands. It is only in south-eastern Australia though that you see them in flocks of thousands, deafening, dazzling and, to a farmer pestilential white cockatoos.

They are large birds, the adult almost 500 mm in length including the tail, with a mobile yellow crest which he raises in alarm, surprise or as a tool in communication, rather in the way that an Italian or a Frenchman talks with his hands. His feathers are pristine white, the undersides of the wings and the cheek feathers tinged with yellow and his eyes dark brown or black. Both sexes have the same plumage so that it is hard to distinguish the cock bird from the hen. This frequently leads to a bird long assumed to be male suddenly surprising its owners with an egg, and many pet cockatoos have had to adapt to a gender-adjusted name in their middle age.

Every flock of cockatoos has its roosting site in eucalypts close to water and from these sites they travel long distances to feed, their main diet being seeds, the legitimate seeds of wild grass, the seeds of bushes and trees or the illegitimate seeds of newly sown crops. These latter they regard as having been provided for their special benefit and they will ignore all natural food, however plentiful, in order to do justice to newly sown oats or maize. They have a carnivorous edge to their appetites as well, eating small insects or larvae in the bark of trees and in captivity occasional extras of wholemeal toast or dry biscuits are gratefully received.

Their breeding season runs from August through to January in Victoria and they nest in hollow branches or holes in the tree-trunks, usually laying two white eggs which are incubated for about 30 days, both sexes doing duty in the sitting. The chicks stay in the nest for about six weeks, adding a plaintive under-whine to the appalling din of the roosting site when the flock is in residence. To live near a roosting site would be a nightmare. The flock leaves at sunrise to find food, every bird having its say at top register, and although they are absent during the day they return, equally vocal, in the evening to post-mortem the day's events until well after dark. To compete with cockatoo noise is useless; Valium and earmuffs are the only answer. They feed during the morning, rest in trees during the heat of midday and feed again in the late afternoon.

The White cockatoo is protected by law, although badly persecuted farmers are sometimes inclined to trap or shoot them in self-defence, and their export overseas is forbidden, except under permit. As a consequence they command huge prices in foreign countries and the incentive for smugglers is always present, a challenge to the Customs Department which makes a valiant effort to catch offenders. The poaching and smuggling of any living creature is totally unacceptable; they are subjected to hideous conditions, and many of them die terrible deaths to satisfy human greed.

In spite of some habits which can only be classed as anti-social the White cockatoo is a bird of intellect and individuality, though if you ask any crop farmer what he thinks of them his language will surprise you. This is understandable because they descend on his newly sown paddocks in immense numbers, meticulously picking up the seed and eating it, strutting along the furrows like little white vacuum cleaners before rising into the air and wheeling off to decimate another crop. White cockatoos may be protected by law, but to men on the land the only good cockatoo is a dead cockatoo, and when crops are newly sown the sound of an approaching flock arouses black fury and despair. On the other hand, the farmer's opinion of cockatoos en masse bears no relation to the infinite pleasure and amusement that many people have enjoyed with a domesticated bird.

In his natural state, wheeling noisily through the air with his mates, the cockatoo is always busy at something, eating, playing or shredding trees just for the hell of it. On his own in captivity he can be a delight, provided he has your company and attention and his natural talent for destruction is kept under control. Bored, caged and ignored he will pine and grow savage, but treated as a member of the family he will become just that. He will learn readily the worst language you can teach him and use it at unsuitable moments, acquire snatches of songs, a human vocabulary which you may deplore and develop a sometimes questionable sense of humour. The tragedy of the pet cockatoo is that so many people buy them without having the least idea what they are taking on.

For a start your cockatoo will almost certainly outlive you. Their life span may extend into their eighties and if you are truly fond of your bird you must make provision for him in your Will. The cockatoo is by nature noisy; his screech is as natural to him as talking is to you, and it is no use getting angry with him when he screeches. Too many people acquire a cockatoo with the vague idea that it will be an undemanding decoration in their home and the inevitable result of this is that very shortly they are trying desperately to get rid of it. This isn't easy; Tehree has more of these discarded cockatoos offered to her than she can house and zoos are in the same boat. People who imagine that they can simply release a house cockatoo should realise that they would be kinder to have it put down, because after a period in captivity it will have no idea how to survive on its own. If it joins a flock of wild cockatoos, which many people believe to be an ideal solution, the established males will think it's after their females and bite the top half of its beak off. Then, of course, it will starve.

Tehree had a call recently from a woman who implored her to take a cockatoo which she said had been with her mother for a long time. 'Mother's had to go into a Home and I've been looking after it, she made me promise to take care of it but I can't stand the thing. It's got to go.'

'How old is it?' Tehree asked.

'It's seventy-three. I know because my parents had had it for ten years when I was born and I'm sixty-three. If you can't take it I'll just have to let it go and then what can I tell mother?'

Tehree's mind boggled at the thought of a seventy-three year-old bird, who could probably no longer even fly, being released into the wild. 'Have it put down', she said. 'It would be much kinder.'

'Oh, I could never face mother again! I promised her!' Tehree, with cockatoos coming out of her ears, agreed to take it.

In 1958, on my way through Frankston market I saw a baby cockatoo in a cage, so young that he was only half-fledged, his beak still pink and soft. The laws regarding wildlife were less stringent then but still, he should never have been on sale. I bought him, took him home and raised him. He was christened Edward Bird, caged only at night or when we were out, and he gave us all immense and lasting joy. He no longer lives with me but with my nephew near Keith in South Australia, because I moved from the country to town. Cockatoo voices at close quarters are a taste few urban neighbours acquire, and my urban neighbours live close by.

Edward was a good example of a bird raised outside his natural environment. Although he was frequently at liberty in the garden he flew reluctantly and without confidence, as if he was merely attempting some foreign skill, and when he flew for any distance he panicked and shouted for rescue. Even when we lived at Kilmore and wild cockatoos often arrived in huge flocks, rioting round Edward's aviary and urging him to join them, he was manifestly appalled. They were alien birds, scary, and he wanted none of them. He went underground, digging long tunnels in the earth of the aviary floor with his beak and claws and retreated into them like a rabbit.

He was very proud of his tunnels. When visitors came he'd strut to the latest tunnel entrance, put up his crest and bounce up and down a few times making appropriate remarks such as, 'Goodbye, Edward Bird!' then dive inside, turning to poke his head out for applause. On hot days he spent long hours under the earth which was cooler than even the shade of the aviary's trees, only coming out when he was called. I have no idea where his tunnel-building skills came from; as far as I know underground engineering is not a common cockatoo talent and these were constructed with immense skill.

Cockatoos have long memories. Three years after I'd taken him to my nephew, Tony Campbell, I went there to stay for a night. I'd deliberately avoided visiting Edward earlier because I thought it might upset him. I thought he might still remember me but I wasn't sure. It was almost dark when we arrived at my nephew's property and pulled up in front of the house. Tony had built Edward, and two companion corellas I'd taken over with him, what could only be described as a Bird Palace and it was out of sight at the back of the garden. As soon as I spoke to Tony there was a wild shriek in the distance, 'Robin, Robin, Robin!' We went straight to the Palace and when I went in he flew into my arms, his wings spread round me, his claws locked into my jumper and he nibbled my cheek very gently. I suppose a dog might remember for so long, or a horse perhaps. It was heart wrenching to leave Edward again but I know he has a happy life there, and hopefully he'll die there when his time comes, loved to the end.

The Laughing Kookaburra
Dacelo Gigas
The Aboriginal people have a legend about this bird, one that illustrates his importance in their culture. According to the legend his morning laughter is a signal to the Sky People to light the great fire that gives daylight and warmth to the earth. To imitate the kookaburra's laughter is forbidden because the Sky People may take offence and shut down their fire, leaving us in darkness. Kookaburra laughter can be deafening at close quarters but somehow it's always cheering, a very Australian sound. When they chorus, several groups telling the other groups where they are, it's as discordant and spontaneous as a crowd of blokes hearing a good story in a pub. If Australia can be said to have a signature tune in the bush the kookaburra provides it, but if you hear him remember not to imitate him, for the Aboriginals may be right and the sun may go out forever.

In more prosaic terms the kookaburra, the largest of all the Kingfisher family, is a bird with an effective social system and a unique, laughing call which advertises his territory. His habitat is in wooded country, usually close to open ground where there is good hunting to satisfy his carnivorous tastes, ranging from invertebrates through insects and rodents to small snakes. The kookaburra is a strong, solid bird, the adult measuring about 400 mm, and with a powerful beak of about 65 mm he can deal with quite large prey. He's an attractive fellow with a white head and stomach, large brown eyes, grey and blue mottled wings and blue rump and a white, brown and black-barred tail. There's a certain fat, cuddly air about a kookaburra sitting on a branch, the look of a kindly children's toy which is sadly deceptive, as anyone who has tangled with its beak will tell you.

The kookaburra pairs for life and, like the magpie, lives in family groups which occupy the same territory all year round, a territory which it is at great pains to defend against other groups. His call is an advertisement to others that his territory is occupied, and other groups reply in the same vein. They may live to twenty years or more, rarely raising more than one clutch a year because the process of rearing the young, a shared, family affair, is so protracted compared to that of most other birds. The female bird lays two or three eggs which are incubated for 24 days, the hatchlings take 36 days to fledge and are fed by their parents and also by the other young family birds, for another eight to thirteen weeks.

When the young reach maturity they usually stay with the family group, helping with the defence of the group's territory and in looking after the younger offspring, for about four years. These auxiliary birds may form one-third of the group's population and because they take up space potentially available to breeders they reduce the group's birth rate by a third. On the other hand, they make themselves extremely useful. Thirty-two per cent of the incubation of new clutches, the brooding of the hatchlings, and sixty per cent of their feeding is attended to by these young family members, making life considerably easier for the parent birds. Any ambition the youngsters may have to breed themselves is firmly suppressed by their elders, until one of the established breeders dies and a space is available. By the time the younger birds are allowed to breed they are fully experienced in child- care and defensive tactics. The kookaburra's predators are few and the risks to his survival small, though destruction of habitat or misuse of pesticides could threaten them in particular areas. In times of an insect plague, such as a locust swarm, they help greatly by gorging themselves on the pest.

The kookaburra can live almost anywhere that provides trees with suitable hollows in which they can nest, and open hunting ground. Their preferred habitat is eastern Australia, particularly the wooded coastal area, but they have been introduced into south-western Australia and Tasmania, both of which seem much to their liking. They appreciate human donations of chopped meat and will become quite tame if these are offered on a regular basis, a labour-saving, opportunistic tendency that might lead one to suspect them of laziness.

Whether from poor eyesight or faulty navigation kookaburras seem particularly prone to collisions with cars. This is all too often the end of them, but many are merely knocked out and recover after a short rest. I was called out to collect such a kookaburra one day by a kindly old couple into whose car it had flown, causing them much distress. They said they'd bedded it down in a cardboard carton and covered it with a towel to keep it quiet until I arrived, and I congratulated them on doing exactly the right thing. When I went into their house, which was white, immaculate and very small, I was shown into the living room, shoe-box size but filled with their treasures, china, pottery and glass, a lifetime's collectibles and the walls smothered with pictures. It was the kind of room that only the owners could love, but for them it was priceless. The carton with the kookaburra inside it stood in the middle of the floor.

'Thank goodness you've come!' said the old lady. 'We couldn't help it, he flew right into our windscreen, poor fellow.'

I said, 'Of course you couldn't help it. Did you notice if there was any blood coming out of its beak?'

The husband said he didn't think so. 'It's out cold though,' he told me. 'I had a look just a minute ago.'

Reassured by this I knelt down by the carton and went to move the towel, but as I touched it the kookaburra returned to consciousness and exploded in uninhibited flight. It was an adult bird and its wingspan in the cluttered little room might have been that of a giant condor. Pictures were swept from the wall, tiny junk-covered tables crashed to the floor, the old lady screamed and her husband used language unbefitting a senior citizen. I tried to get the towel over the frantic bird who was circuiting the room like a demon, and knocked more treasures over. There was only one thing to do, I flung their front window open, pushed out the fly wire and by sheer good luck the kookaburra found the opening and disappeared. Two shattered old people stared at the rubble that had once been their lifetime memories and there was nothing I could do or say to comfort them. Since then I have never tried to examine a bird or an animal until I have it in a safe and suitable environment, and I doubt if the old people have ever tried to be kind to another kookaburra.

The Australian Magpie
Gymnorhina tibicen

The early British settlers in Australia, who were inclined to be contemptuous of this new, uncivilised land, claimed that our flowers had no scent and our birds had no song. They kept on dragging up skylarks and nightingales in nostalgic comparison but they must have been selectively deaf to dismiss our birds so arbitrarily. They may have had a case about the flowers for no doubt they'd never smelled boronia then, but they can hardly have failed to hear our birds. The Australian magpie, one of our commonest and most underrated birds, can burst into a dawn chorus of liquid melody, a song of pure, wild exaltation more lovely, I swear, than any skylark. The magpie is a misjudged bird, credited with a malignant nature because of its tendency to dive-bomb people who approach its nest in springtime. This is a David and Goliath gesture considering the relative sizes of them and us, and the magpie should be respected, not blamed for it. A magpie's home is his castle and he's quite entitled to see off potential intruders. He's also a talented mimic and, given sufficient proximity to humans, he can talk.

Magpies live in closely-knit family groups and the dominant male defends the family's territory with great ferocity. The fledglings are encouraged out of the nest quite early so that, supervised by the parent birds, they can learn about feeding themselves, develop their muscles and grow their adult plumage. At this stage they're unsteady on their feet and perpetually grizzling for the food which has hitherto been supplied by their mother. Kindly people, finding them on the ground in apparent distress, are apt to imagine, because of their whining and unsteadiness that they're abandoned, pick them up and hand them in to care. In a nearby tree the magpie parents, who have been bringing up their child according to magpie lore, watch this unnecessary abduction in helpless consternation. Tehree has hundreds of baby magpies brought to her every spring and many of these, she says, should have been left where they were found.

'People see a young magpie lurching about on the ground and they think it's helpless. It's not helpless at all, it's just like a small child learning to walk and its family's keeping an eye on it all the time. When they are picked up and brought to Jirrahlinga we keep them in groups according to the area they've come from, then release them in that same area when they're old enough. They go out in groups of up to ten, mainly females and a couple of males. Magpies live as families so that way the group can form a new family of their own.'

Occasionally you will come across a Special Magpie, Special because they choose to live with people, never caged or coerced in any way, free to fly wherever and whenever they wish. At Kilmore there was Maud. Our large vegetable garden there, being fenced and roofed with cyclone wire, was a perfect nursery for the baby magpies which were brought to me with monotonous regularity in the springtime. In spring there were never less than half a dozen little black and white monsters, whining for food-on-demand. They were usually ready for release about Christmas time, having flown freely round the 10 metre long, 4 metre high vegetable garden-cum-cage and learned about worms the natural way. One year there was a baby magpie, a female, who was different from the rest. From the beginning she wanted personal attention, fluttered into your lap and nibbled the dogs' noses through the wire with evident affection. When release time came the others flew off but Maud, as she'd already been named, walked out through the gate on her two feet, joined our three dogs and started barking.

Maud, having decided to be a dog, automatically came into the house when the dogs did and accepted our two cats as they accepted her, lying on her back on the carpet between their paws or at times perching on their backs. If she was somewhere else when the other animals came into the house she would knock on the window with her beak until it was opened for her. Strange dogs never stayed around for long; Maud terrorised them by flying just above their heads like a small jet fighter, pecking with great accuracy, and barking. I think her bark was the ultimate terror for them. It was loud and very dog-like yet they could see no dog and large, bloodthirsty mongrels fled our garden howling, never to return. The baby 'roos and wombats that came and went never questioned her of course, and she was infinitely gentle with them but it was our Jack Russells that she loved. She spent most of her time with them, outside or in, and when they rushed out barking to greet a visitor Maud flew out, barking too. If she was tired or feeling lazy she'd lie on her back in my lap, claws in the air, and sleep. The dogs lay on our laps at times so why not Maud, who barked as well as they did and knew she was at least half dog.

I have talked of the morning song of magpies, the wonderful exuberant music that spills down from the height of the trees. Maud would often stand, legs braced, on the back of a chair or a sofa or even flat-footed on the carpet, and break into song as though it was a present to us from her, rapture laid at our feet because we were her family. Tragically Maud died when she was only five years old. She had developed a red-worm aneurism which affects horses as well as magpies and can be fatal in both. We missed her horribly; she had chosen us of her own will, and the privilege was entirely ours. A magpie is essentially free, it belongs to the wind and the trees. A Special Magpie is born, not made, and those of us who have known one have been blessed.

For a long time the Australian magpie was in something of a scientific muddle because it was thought to consist of three species, the black-backed, the white-backed and the Western magpie. Then it was found that all three interbred freely and therefore all our magpies belong to the same species. 'Magpie' is an imported Pommy name for an Australian bird that has no relationship at all to the English magpie who, in fact, belongs to the crow family. There is a remote physical resemblance in that they both have black and white plumage but our magpie, in my opinion, is a far more interesting bird. Anyone who has taken the time to watch them, or to listen to their superb song will appreciate that they are among our most valuable species. The Australian magpie is found all over the continent except in the far north and it is aggressively territorial. All the members of a magpie family help to defend their territory, not only from other birds but from threats on the ground, humans and dogs included. Their method of dive-bombing is accurate and intimidating and there are few two-legged Aussies who have not at some time retreated, their hands protecting their skulls from an enraged male magpie.

The female magpie literally gets the short end of the stick for she must build the nest, a large, woven basket of twigs, without help,

Maud had convinced herself that she was a dog.

and then rely on the dominant male of the group to feed her while she incubates the eggs for 20 days. Because the male bird's first priority is the defence of his family territory this is a hungry, anxious time for the female and although there may be several occupied nests the male will only feed one female bird. As a result it is rare for more than one nest to produce hatchlings. The dominant male usually fathers all the broods in the group, although accidents may happen when his back is turned and some feathered bounder sneaks in to steal a mating.

The juvenile period of learning is much the most dangerous chapter in a magpie's life because of its time on the ground, and inevitably many of them don't survive. A study of 37 groups of magpies showed that from one breeding season the survivors a year later numbered only one per group, but on the whole those that do survive are the strongest of their kind, and it's unlikely there'll ever be a shortage of magpies in our trees. Man's clearing and development of the Australian countryside has had two opposing effects on these birds. On the good side an increase in the availability of food, worms, grubs and insects in the open ground; on the down side a decrease in the trees they need for roosting and breeding. No-one would suggest at this stage that magpies are a threatened species; my own view is that they are tougher than we are, that in spite of us they'll find a way to survive.

The Emu
Dromaius novaehollandiae

There are many facets to our large, flightless compatriot, some admirable and some, if you happen to be a wheat farmer for instance, diabolic. He is nomadic, omnivorous, incurably inquisitive and, if you happen to be a militant feminist, altogether the ideal working husband.

The mating birds form pairs in December and January and stay together for about five moths The female lays her eggs in May, usually a clutch of between 7 and 11 but sometimes considerably more. Even before she's finished laying her mate is fussing around the clutch, impatient to start incubating the new generation. The female, having finished laying, simply wanders off to fritter away her time with other emu ladies, while the male grits his beak and endures eight long weeks of continuous sitting, hardly leaving the nest even to feed. He suffers serious weight loss during this incubation period, perhaps as much as 8 kg, nor do his duties finish there. When the chicks hatch he must lead them around, brood them under his feathers and generally act as both mother and father for as much as eighteen months. This paternal devotion means that for him the next breeding season is a write-off and he must wait two years between one mating and the next.

Emus inhabit most areas of Australia but rise to plague proportions in the wheatlands of the west, This resulted in the famous Western Australian Emu War of 1932, when a detachment of soldiers with two Lewis guns were sent to wipe them out. The flat, barren landscape must have reeled under the noise, the dust and the bullets but when it all died down 10,000 rounds of ammunition had been wasted, for the emus were still there.

Their curiosity is enormous and the Aboriginals, who were excessively fond of emu meat, exploited it to catch them. A man would climb a tree with a bunch of rags and emu feathers on a string and twirl it round, an irresistible attraction to nearby emus who rushed to see it. The man in the tree would spear them from above and the subsequent commotion would bring more inquisitive birds to share their fate.

The diversity of the emu diet ensures their survival in all but the most catastrophic droughts. They will eat seeds, grass, the flowers and fruit of native plants, herbs and insects according to availability and season. In certain regions they have annual migrations, to the south-west in spring and the north-east in autumn, often over long distances.

Jirrahlinga has its share of emus. One of their birds came to them after house-raising with a family, an educated, humanised emu who had even learned to sit on command. A new trainee, still nervous of wildlife, was silly enough to be cheeky to the staff and as a punishment was told to 'go and clean the emu's teeth.' Emus struck her as oversized and potentially deadly so, shaking with fear, she donned a long, heavy white coat, a tin hat and looking rather like a World War II air raid warden she advanced on the emu. Fearing for her life she entered the enclosure whereat the emu, wanting to be friends, sat down in front of her and she knelt to be on the same level as its teeth. Stretching out her arms and saying her prayers she made her first basic discovery about emus. They have no teeth.

Raptors

These are the hunters of our skies, the silhouettes we see hanging motionless, high on the air currents, then diving with streamlined accuracy on their prey. They range from kites and falcons, goshawks and peregrines through to eagles, all carnivorous, all possessing the gift of unbelievable, telescopic eyesight and soaring, effortless flight. They choose their prey according to its relative size and strength but are not above scavenging when the opportunity occurs. The Wedgetail eagle, who can have a wing span of 2.5 metres and is a relation of the Northern Hemisphere's Golden eagle, is Australia's largest bird of prey.

For a long time our Wedgie, his name inevitably shortened in line with Australian custom, had an undeservedly bad reputation among sheep farmers. He was supposed to hunt and kill young lambs, and the farmers responded by conducting a vendetta against the eagle, shooting him on sight. There were apocryphal stories about the

Wedgie, one that even credited an eagle with killing a horse, but in a recent study it was established that eagles do very little damage to stock. Most of the lambs they feed on are either sickly or already dead and their favourite diet is of rabbits, young wallabies or kangaroos, reptiles or rodents. One hopes that once farmers are convinced of this the Wedgetail will be safe from their guns, because our skies would be the sadder for their absence.

Wedgetail eagles sometimes arrive injured at Jirrahlinga, awe-inspiring in their size and power. They can be treated for their injuries, with caution and by experts, but the priority is to get them back to the area where they were found as soon as possible. You will seldom see a singleton Wedgetail because they pair for life, and somewhere the injured bird's mate will be waiting for its return.

Tehree quotes the case of a young female that had flown into a barbed wire fence and been badly torn. 'The man who brought her here saw it happen. She'd swooped down after her prey and flown into the fence at full speed. When she'd recovered we asked around in the district where he'd found her and there was a place where a pair of eagles had been seen together over the past few months, so we took her there to release her. It was wonderful to see her soar again and she kept calling her mate as she went higher and higher, but he didn't come. Then a few days later a farmer came to say he'd seen the two of them flying together again and that season they produced two chicks.

'Feeding raptors is a challenge because you need to know whether they feed on the ground or in flight, on the wing. They're opportunist feeders – they may catch a good meal and then not have another for some time – so they eat as much as they can, when they can. We offer them a feed as soon as we get them in case they're hungry, and we weigh them. All zoos and carers have a weight chart for raptors and it's important to make sure their weight's right before release. A raptor in captivity needs a diet that contains roughage because his natural prey would have hair or feathers, and without these or a suitable substitute combined with his meat his inside won't function. He also needs supplementary calcium to compensate for the bone fragments he swallows when he's tearing at the bird or mammal he has killed in the wild.

This picture shows how to hold a raptor with one hand: the tail, talons and wing tips of this Goshawk are all held fast, enabling the bird to be examined. (The hand, as it happens, is Tehree's.)

'You must be very careful of their talons when you handle them, they're razor sharp and they can grab you quick as a flash. Once they've grabbed you they hang on and most people automatically pull away, so that the bird thinks you're trying to escape and grips harder. Keep away from the talons, but if you do get caught by them you must try to relax. It's not easy but it's the only thing to do. Raptors, all of them, need expert knowledge and handling, and if you get one you should hand it over to someone who's experienced in caring for them, as soon as possible.'

Tehree has various species of raptor brought to her by people who have found them with broken legs, wings or some other form of injury, most of them goshawks or peregrines, or the smaller falcons. The broken legs and wings can be set, other injuries mended and the bird released, but far too often there's a worse problem. According to Tehree many of the raptors that come to her have been kept too long in a small cage, often in a wire cage, and have irreparable feather damage. The plumage of a bird that soars on the air, as raptors must do to see their prey, has a complex and indispensable system of feathers without which it is flightless. While an expert can sometimes repair the damage by clipping and grafting the feathers, often enough the bird must be put down. The answer to the problem is to hang shade-cloth or some other fabric on the inside of the cage so that the bird can't batter its feathers against the wire in an effort to get out.

Falconry, the practice of training certain varieties of the raptor family to hunt prey on the wing for their masters, is an art as much as it is a sport, and probably the closest relationship man has ever formed with these birds. It has been practiced since time immemorial and is still well loved by the oil-rich Sheiks of the Middle East. The art lies in the care and training of the birds, for raptors are a proud breed who do not submit readily to humans and at best to only one, the man who has earned their trust. The training of falcons was a skill handed down through generations of the same families, and in the days of Henry VIII the falconer was an important fellow. Falconry was a Sport of Kings in Europe then, of prancing horses and feathered hats, with bejewelled ladies mounted on palfreys, admiring from a safe distance. A Royal Falconer would have guarded his secrets from all but his sons. Over the centuries these secrets have largely been lost and the sport forgotten in Europe, surviving now only among the men of the deserts where it all began.

The Silver Gull
Larus novaehollandiae

Everybody loves a penguin but not necessarily a Silver Gull, that grey, greedy, grumpy citizen of our beaches that we know as a common seagull. Tehree, however, is a gull fan. 'They're so tough,' she says. 'Think of the conditions they live through on the sea and the way they can survive almost anything. Of course they're bad-tempered, they have to fight for everything just to live. You'll often see a seagull with only one leg but he's still as fit and brave and determined as any of the others. Very few people have ever seen a seagull chick so sometimes they bring them to us, not knowing what they are. They look like a little round, brown-speckled balls of fluff, not like a seagull at all, but they grow into a lovely, streamlined seabird.'

We all know them so well that we almost cease to notice them; they flock on our rubbish dumps, our paddocks, our playing fields and indeed anywhere they can find food, from the coasts to inland Australia. They are migratory birds, the stronger individuals travelling for greater distances than the weaker ones, those that breed on the Victorian lakes ranging as far as Woomera.

Their preferred breeding sites are on bare ground where they build a platform nest out of whatever material they can find, lining it with softer foliage or grass. If bare ground is scarce they will make do with shrubs, dead trees or the banks of rivers or dams, and on some coastal islands they have started erosion by destroying the vegetation. The male bird establishes the nesting territory and is joined by a female, usually his previous mate, and they share the nest building, raising two to four chicks who become independent at six weeks.

Silver Gulls exist in their enormous numbers largely because of their genius for adaptability to climate, to location, to food and in fact to almost anything the world can throw at them. Love them or hate them the Silver Gulls are among the great survivors of this world and, like Tehree, we should take off our hats to them.

The Australian Pelican
Pelicanus conspicillatus

Pelicans are brought in to Jirrahlinga with a variety of injuries, the strangest of these being one that had an arrow passing right through it from one side to the other. 'There are always lots of pelicans around here, on the river and in the wetlands,' Tehree says. 'I suppose some kid with a bow and arrow had taken a shot at this one. We made sure that the arrow hadn't touched anything vital inside the bird, then cut the arrowhead off, covered the shaft with anti-biotic and pulled it out. The anti-biotic covered the wound inside the bird as the shaft came through and it recovered perfectly.

'When Pelicans are hunting in the water they use the pouch, or lower mandible, under their bill as a kind of fishing net. There was a pelican that was recuperating on our pond where one of our ducks had just hatched out a family of ducklings. One of the staff came to me and said, "We've got ten ducklings on the pond," and I said, "Good, I must come and see."

'We went down to the pond and I counted and found there were only nine so we started to hunt round for the tenth. When we turned back to the pond there were only eight and I noticed the pelican sailing along in the water behind them. As I watched he dipped his bill into the pond and another duckling vanished. The man with me grabbed the pelican, forced his bill open and plunged his arm in. He got two of the ducklings back alive out of the bird's pouch, but the first one it had taken was too far gone, and it died.'

Pelicans breed all over Australia, wherever there are lakes or streams, and along our shores. I have seen them in large numbers on Cooper's Creek, about as far as you can get from the sea, but as much at home as they'd be in an ocean environment. On inland rivers they hunt in formation to drive the fish into the shallows, all dipping their bills into the water at the same time and raising them slightly open so that the water drains out of the pouch, leaving the fish to be swallowed. Even at sea pelicans prefer calm water, probably because their method of taking off from water is ponderous in the extreme and in rough seas it would be nearly impossible. It involves laborious flapping of wings and churning of feet for some distance before lift-off is achieved, but there is then a transformation into effortless flight in

This very lethal-looking arrow was sticking right through the pelican, but it made a total recovery.

which they can use thermals as an eagle does, and soar up to 3000 m.

The pelican's domestic arrangements are admirably shared. They become sexually mature as four-year-olds, when they gather at a breeding site and their bills change colour to advertise their readiness for mating. The front two-thirds of the bill turns scarlet and the underside pink with a dark line on each side. After they pair up the colour fades, except for the dark line which turns red. Pairing consists of several males following a female until only one male is left, after which they both collect nesting material, the female from near the nesting site and the male doing the harder, more distant work. The actual building of the nest is a joint effort as is the incubation of the two snow-white eggs, shared in 10 hour shifts which allows the non-sitting bird time to feed. The young hatch in 30 to 35 days and both parents combine in feeding them for three months.

Pelican chicks have violent convulsions after feeding, flapping and biting at anything near them like rabid dogs, then collapsing on the ground after a minute or so. This alarming display is thought to be an elaborate form of begging, presumably for more food, and one suspects that none but a parent pelican would put up with such importunate offspring. Considering their domestic wisdom, their adaptability and versatility, it's a wonder pelicans haven't taught their children better manners.

The Australasian Gannet
Morus serrator

This is a large and lovely sea bird, a native both of the southern coastline of Australia and of New Zealand. Its nesting sites are generally on rocky islands off the coast, but in Port Phillip Bay they also make use of man-made platforms such as West Light, a navigation beacon off Queenscliff, and during their breeding season Jirrahlinga inevitably has an intake of rescued baby gannets.

On their breeding sites the parent birds indulge in serious overcrowding. Each bird builds its nest, made of guano and debris, on about a square metre of territory. As their wingspan can measure up to two metres and there is a great deal of jostling and noisy argument among the adults, the babies get pushed off the platform into the water. There, though they can float, predators or starvation would soon put an end to them unless they're lucky enough to be rescued.

'A baby gannet's just a white ball of fluff,' Tehree says. 'Sometimes you can't even find where the head is. The feathers come right over their eyes and they have to puff it away when they want to see and when they get pushed into the water they float like thistledown. Don't ever take a baby gannet lightly though, their beaks are sharp as razors even at that stage. The adult's beak is worse because it's bigger; an adult gannet can slice you open in one second.

'When the babies are brought in we have to be very careful feeding them. One person has to hold the beak open while another one stuffs little pieces of fish into it. The staff always seem to make themselves scarce when it's baby gannet feeding time. The birds gradually learn to feed themselves and then we have to start getting them ready for release, putting them in an enclosure with conditions as close as possible to those they'll be going back to. We feed them well to build up their muscle tone, and when they're really strong and healthy we take them for a free boat ride, courtesy of our volunteers, and return them to their original home. We take them back as soon as possible, and it's amazing to see them find their own parents in that crowd of other birds.

'The juveniles go through a second growth stage when they shed their fluff and turn a rather unattractive grey, but it's really a protective camouflage while they're growing up. The adult birds are lovely, white with a yellow head, black primary feathers and a slate-blue throat stripe, males and females both the same.

'The really spectacular thing is to see gannets dive for fish in the sea. They spot the fish when they're about ten metres off the water, fold back those great wings so that they're shaped like an arrow head and then just plummet straight down. They dive at tremendous speed so nature's given them a kind of percussion pad on the top of their heads to cushion the shock when they hit the water. A flock of gannets hunting a school of fish is a marvellous sight – they actually herd the fish, some gannets on the water, others in the air, spearing down in turn to seize their fish and soar back up again.'

The Fairy Penguin

Eudyptula minor

Of all the eighteen species of penguin in the Southern Hemisphere ours is the smallest, and the only one to breed on Australian shores. It is also known as the Little Penguin, and it has become famous among tourists who come from distant places to watch the Penguin Parade at night on a Phillip Island beach, when the birds return to the dunes after a day in the sea. The penguins of Phillip Island have become blasé about tourists and flashbulbs, regarding both as a harmless, inescapable part of their bedtime ritual. In their innocence they don't connect people with oil spills.

There are plenty of things that threaten a small penguin in the sea, almost everything bigger than itself in fact, and life was dangerous enough for them before oil tankers came along but at least their perils were natural. Now, in addition to their aquatic predators we face these birds with a new enemy, against which they are helpless unless we can reach the victims in time and clean them. Over the years Tehree has built up a network of people, pilots and others, who notify her of threats to seabirds such as oil slicks, giving her time to mobilise for the flood of birds-in-need-of-help which will inevitably follow. It means that volunteer helpers must be called in because when birds are covered in oil there's no time to lose, and the birds may arrive in hundreds. Our oil clogs and destroys the natural oil in their feathers so that the birds cannot swim

'We've had more than our share of these oiled birds from the coast here,' Tehree says. 'We have a set routine for cleaning them up. First of all we have to be very careful when we handle them because the oil can be very toxic to humans – you mustn't get it on your skin and for the same reason you mustn't let the bird preen itself and swallow the stuff. We wash the oil off the bird as quickly as possible, wearing rubber gloves. We use a dishwashing liquid called Dawn, but some brands are actually harmful so be careful what you use, then dry the bird and keep it warm, out of draughts. It may take more than one wash to really clean off the oil and you mustn't let it preen itself until it's completely clean

'With penguins that have been in oil and washed we put cardboard discs on their beaks so they can't open them to preen themselves, and dress them in little ponchos or knitted jumpers to keep them warm. It's lovely sight; a lot of penguins waddling round in their little jumpers, often in football club colours. The jumpers are knitted by kind ladies in various women's organisations. We always have a stock of these jumpers on hand for emergencies.

'After the bird's cleaned you must allow it time to waterproof itself again before it goes back to the sea. The natural oils in a seabird's skin enable it to float and keep it warm. These oils restore naturally but without them the bird will get hypothermia or drown. The waterproofing may take some time, days or even weeks, but you can tell when it has waterproofed itself again by putting it in a bath of water for a moment and seeing if it rides on the surface or sinks.

'You should take a sample of the oil on its feathers and get it analysed to find out exactly what kind of oil it is. Notify the local authorities about any oil slick in case they don't know, so that they can clean it up. Another thing to remember is not to pour the washed-off oil down the sink because it may get into the ground water and poison it. We pour the polluted water onto sand where the oil gets absorbed.

'Penguins turn up in odd places, very often because some half-

SAVING AN OIL-SOAKED PENGUIN

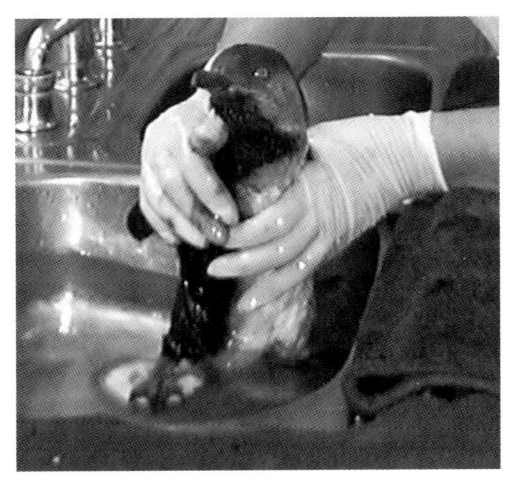

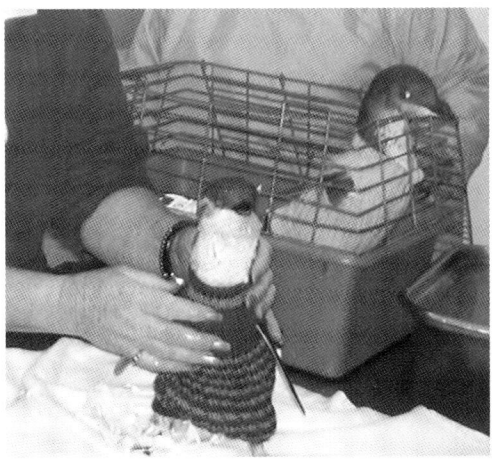

The oil is washed off, using a detergent. The detergent removes the natural oil as well, and until this is restored the penguin is kept warm with a knitted jumper.

Once they have recovered their natural oils, the penguins go to the rehab ward. When taken to the beach for release, the penguins are at first bewildered

Then instinct takes over and they gather in a bunch and head for the sea. Somebody has to be last in.

wit has picked them up on the beach and carried them off. I had a call from the McDonald's at Belmont, miles away from the coast asking me to collect a penguin, and I found it in the children's play area with a party hat on. It was quite okay otherwise and it had a good fish supper when it got to Jirrahlinga.

'Then there was a guy who'd been partying on the beach with some friends. He rang me in the middle of the night to say they'd found some penguins "lost" in the sand dunes. Penguins lost in sand dunes, for God's sake! They were just camping for the night. He and his friends had "rescued" them and put them in their cars and were trying to find someone to look after them and what should he do? I couldn't believe anyone was that silly so I said, "Tell your friends to take them back to the beach and let them go, then go home yourselves and let the penguins and everyone else get some sleep." I suppose he meant well. A lot of people think that when a penguin's found on land it's in some kind of trouble, but in fact they spend a lot of time there. By the same token they can travel incredible distances in the sea. The practice of banding penguins has shown us just how far they go. Two penguins banded in Tasmania later turned up in Sydney Harbour.'

The busiest time of the Fairy Penguin year is the breeding season, lasting from July to November or December in Victoria. The male returns to the breeding site first and is joined by the female, usually his wife from the previous season, and they either go back to their old burrow or create a new one, with a nest chamber lined with plant material. The female lays two white eggs and both parents share in their incubation, one parent sitting and the other going to the sea to feed, their shifts sometimes lasting up to ten days. If the first clutch of eggs fails to hatch they may lay again and can even raise two clutches of young in one season.

When the eggs hatch the parents alternate guarding and feeding duties every night until the chicks are about two weeks old. After that the demand for food forces both parents to spend the day catching fish, then scrambling up the beach with bulging tummies to regurgitate the fish directly into the beaks of their young. When the chicks finally leave, the parents, thin and exhausted, go to sea for about six weeks to recuperate, returning fat, restored in mind and body and ready to moult. During the moulting period, which may take two to three weeks, the adults remain on shore.

The Cape Barren Goose
Cereopsis novaehollandiae

This portly, pugnacious bird came close to extinction in the early days of settlement, when they and their eggs were hunted for food by the sealing industry workers in Bass Strait. If we had lost them it would have been a tragedy for they are unique, not only as birds of great character but as a puzzle to scientists who, unable to classify them as true geese, have put them in a subspecies of their own. They are found only in Australia and are among the least numerous breed of waterfowl in the world.

Tehree has Cape Barren geese at Jirrahlinga, one in particular who marches round inside the koala enclosure, inspecting each visitor with the air of one who has long since decided that humans are inferior. Tehree fell in love with them when she saw a bunch of white, fluffy chicks blown along the ground in a strong wind. They righted themselves and fought their way back to their mother against the gale, thereby displaying the Cape Barren's inbuilt determination at an early age. Their fighting spirit develops as they grow and parent geese will attack anything that approaches their young. They are usually found in pairs and are thought to mate for life, the male helping with nest building, a shallow cup made with whatever's to hand and lined with grey down, and he defends their territory while the female is brooding. The family keeps to their territory, feeding on plants until the young are six weeks old, when the parents abandon them and the juveniles form groups with others of their own age.

Paired Cape Barren Geese are aggressively territorial, especially during the breeding season, and flocks still occur in great numbers on the Bass Strait islands where they were once shot as agricultural pests. They make an annual visit to mainland Australia, although in far smaller numbers than in the past, and as a filly protected species hopefully their numbers will increase.

12 OUTSIDERS

The Dingo

Family *Canidae*

Canis familiaris dingo
Dingoes are not native to Australia; it is believed that they were introduced by the Aborigines, perhaps as much as 8,000 years ago. They are found all over our continent except in Tasmania, presumably reaching the south coast after Tasmania was isolated by the formation of Bass Strait. Before the arrival of the white man their food was native fauna, but since the development of sheep farming they have a new, tempting addition to their diet and they have become the sworn enemy of sheep men. In areas where there are large numbers of dingoes they are shot, poisoned and trapped, automatically blamed for the death of sheep and lambs. This may be unjust because there is some doubt about the amount of damage they actually do to stock which is believed to make up only 2 per cent of their diet. To the dingo's credit he also preys on feral pigs, cats and rabbits, any one of which should be considered a worse pest than the dingo himself. Dingoes pair permanently, raising their young together and breeding only once a year, while the domestic dog breeds twice. They have well-defined home ranges, their location and numbers dependent on the availability of prey. They are solitary hunters when the prey involved is small, but hunt as packs when the quarry is too large for an individual dingo.

    The dog and the dingo belong to the same species and can interbreed quite successfully. Our best cattle dogs, the Queensland Heeler and the Kelpie have dingo blood and both these breeds are tireless, intelligent workers. At the same time they have characteristics which are absent in purely domestic breeds; they are essentially outdoor dogs bred for wide open spaces, and there are times when their dingo ancestry shows through. There are few less comfortable situations than being silently followed at close quarters by a Queensland Heeler whose intentions are suspect, yet both the Heeler and the Kelpie are enormously faithful to the person who owns them. Other dingo crosses can be far less attractive; the packs of feral dogs which roam parts of the country and do horrendous damage to both stock and wildlife are often a mixture of dingo and runaway domestic breeds, combining the worst in both.

There are half a dozen mature dingoes at Jirrahlinga, all of whom have been handed on after an unsuccessful earlier career as a household pet, and Tehree has learned both to read them and to use them. All of them are pure-bred dingoes, and however anyone may argue to the contrary the dingo is a wild animal, not just another breed of domestic dog, therefore the assumption that it can be treated as a normal pet is dangerously wrong. The Australian Canine Association has encouraged their breeding, even running classes for dingoes in dog shows, regardless of the fact that their reactions and temperaments do not conform to accepted canine parameters, and that in a domestic situation they must always constitute a risk.

Tehree's dingoes are kept mainly as an exhibit in the Sanctuary, but there are times when their native ability as trackers comes in very handy indeed. In a Sanctuary the size of Jirrahlinga there are the inevitable times when some animal gets out of its enclosure, finds a hiding place to its liking and vanishes. In the wild its life may depend on concealment, and the ability of a wombat or an echidna to disappear into the one place where you'd never dream of looking for them is astounding. In the case of Jirrahlinga residents, as long as they're at large they're at risk, and they have to be found. Instead of mobilising the entire staff for a time-wasting and probably unsuccessful search, Tehree turns to one of her pure bred dingoes.

'Dingoes don't track as other dogs do, nose to ground, following a scent,' she says, 'They have to literally impregnate themselves with the smell of the animal you want them to find. Say it's a wombat that's got out of its pen. I put the dingo in that same pen and it'll roll about in the earth and the straw that the wombat's been living in, as if it's soaking itself in that wombat's scent. When it's done that for a while I put a tracking harness and a correction collar on it and take it outside. It'll carry its head up, as if the scent's in the wind rather than on the ground, and the funny thing is that it can stop when it's distracted by something else, the 'roos, say, or something alongside, but it'll get going again. An ordinary dog would lose the scent. Then finally it'll stop at a bush or some bit of cover you'd never have thought of, and look at you as if it's saying, 'There you are, that's where it is' and that's where the wombat will be, tucked away where we'd never have found it.'

'An echidna got out of its cage one day. They can claw their way out of anything and we looked everywhere, but finally I had to get the dingo. He rolled himself around in its cage and then I took him out on the harness. He wandered about for a while, like the echidna had probably done, and to my surprise we ended up at the wall of the koala hospital which Hamish was building at the time. There was nothing visible that the echidna could have hidden in and I thought the dingo had lost the plot, so I tried to drag him away, back onto the scent, but he didn't want to come. He kept looking at me, then at the wall again, trying to tell me and probably thinking I was

A dingo pup at Jirrahlinga

stupid. I didn't know Hamish had put a sheet of plaster in as a double wall. We pulled it out and there was the echidna, it had dug its way in and it was wedged right up in the cavity. We'd never have found it on our own.'

The dingo is another case of an animal that acquires a bad name because people treat it in the wrong way. The Azaria Chamberlain case and the recent killing of a small boy on Fraser Island have blackened the dingo's reputation. Both cases were very tragic, but both occurred in areas where dingoes had been encouraged by tourists and campers to enter human territory. 'Look, this dingo's coming quite close to the camp for the scraps I'm throwing to him!' Of course he's coming close, he's hungry and it's easy pickings but it doesn't mean he's turned into a dog or that you've become his friend. You are his natural enemy. In the wild he'd have run from you but you've just turned yourself into a Fast Food dispenser and you've lost his respect. Don't blame the dingo!

The Fox

Vulpes vulpes

The fox, like the dingo, is a foreigner, but a far more recent arrival and a greater villain, as far as our wildlife is concerned. It was introduced to Australia in 1860, and spread like wildfire over all but the far north of the continent and Tasmania. It rapidly became the enemy of the sheep farmer, of anyone who kept poultry and a target for anyone who cared about our environment. The fox can live anywhere that provides it with food and shelter, and Australia is rich in both. Its most unattractive feature is its habit of killing for the joy of killing, not simply because it is in need of food. Tehree, like most Shelter and Sanctuary operators, has had experience of fox massacres, and dreads what they can do, but she still manages to have a good word for them.

'Actually I like foxes as individuals. They're only doing what they're born to do, and it's up to us to control them, one way or the other. We've had terrible trouble with the wild foxes recently and they've killed a lot of our birds, including ducks and Cape Barren geese, and they've even got to the tortoises. It's been traumatic and I estimate we've lost about $15,000 worth of stock.

'We had a fox of our own here for years, a dominant fox, and I used to gather his scats and put them round the boundary. The other foxes would smell them and stay out, knowing it was someone else's territory. I even watched a wild dog fox once, sniffing the scats and then tuning away. Our fox was ill at one time and had to stay at the vet's place, so there were no scats and ten days after he'd left here the feral foxes were back, but when he recovered and the scats were put out again we had no more trouble. Our fox died recently, and ten days later the killings started again. It puzzles me that it takes that ten days each time but maybe the scats have a shelf life as deterrents.

'There's no way you can get rid of all the foxes in this country now, they're too widespread and too hardy. Poisoning is out, as far as I'm concerned, because it kills so many other things, trapping and shooting hardly make a dent in the numbers and the Government authorities themselves are petty disappointing. This is a wetland area, terribly important for all kinds of birds, both native and migratory, but it's stiff with foxes, in spite of the fact that the DNRE were recently granted a large sum of money specifically to eradicate them. The foxes just increase and they'll end up by wiping out the birds. It's estimated that there are twenty foxes per square kilometre round here. The only sensible way to control them is for the Government to declare a $5 a head bounty on them. It would give the gun enthusiasts something useful to do as well.'

Tasmania, that treasury of small, wild creatures now extinct on the mainland, victims of the predators we introduced, was once quite free of foxes, but recently some may have been let loose in its northern bushland. If so this a sin, it's a tragedy and a loss to us all.

PART THREE

JIRRAHLINGA TODAY

In this section, we look at some of the activities at Jirrahlinga – the problems and some of their solutions. If some of it, like the need for euthanasia, sounds pretty grim, that is true. If some of it sounds fascinating and rewarding, that too is true.

Motor car victim. The neck brace is a precaution in case of spinal damage. In this case the koala had severe head injuries.

Release is not just a matter of letting the animals go. Jirrahlinga's possum release program involves careful selection of appropriate release sites, where there is no resident population with prior territorial rights, and some subtle ways of making the possums feel at home.

13 Rescue, Release and Euthanasia

Jirrahlinga's Animal Rescue Service

Jirrahlinga's Animal Rescue Service is one of its most important activities. Wildlife can get into trouble at any time, singly or in droves but, since many are nocturnal, more often than not in the middle of the night and all calls for help must be answered. Daytime situations can frequently be handled by one of the staff, but at night Tehree, however tired she may be, must drag herself out of bed and drive to the scene of the trouble. Sometimes the calls are genuine; at others they are the result of panic, misunderstanding or plain stupidity. Sometimes she can give advice to the caller on the phone and they can manage themselves, but when there is any doubt at all she must go, no matter how late or how far.

Most of the calls for help involve the more common species of birds and mammals, posing the question of whether the rescue and rehabilitation of a single member of such a species is really worthwhile. For Tehree it isn't a question of 'worthwhile' because if any animal, wild or domestic, is in need of help she will help it. She was asked the other day whether, presented with a choice, she'd save an animal belonging to an endangered species before a common animal.

She thought about it for a minute, then said, 'I'd save them both if I could, and they'd both be treated exactly the same at Jirrahlinga. We'd do our best for both of them.'

'But there must be some that you really shouldn't save, some of the introduced species that are known pests. What happens if you get brought a fox, for instance, or a rabbit or a rat?'

'Those would be put down, but we'd give them a good feed first. Whenever anything comes in that's going to be put down it gets a feed before that happens. In some places badly injured and stressed animals are just left in the cold and the dark for hours until they're euthanased and that's cruel, they shouldn't die hungry and frightened.

'Of course there are creatures we wouldn't try to save, if they belong to a pest species. Sometimes people bring us in a baby rat because they think it's a baby possum and we put that down, but we give it a feed first. I would never tell anyone that they've brought us a rat by mistake because I want to encourage the public to care about wildlife. If they believe they've saved something worthwhile they'll be pleased, they'll watch out for other animals to save and encourage other people to do the same. It's a way to get people interested in wildlife, and if they're interested they'll learn. At present amazingly few townspeople know anything much about our native species except what they look like in pictures, and they have totally wrong attitudes to them. They're frightened of them or they think they might be dirty, and scarcely anyone would know what they eat or the kind of habitat they need. Somehow we've got to change all that by educating people, or our wildlife won't survive.

'I get calls from all over the State, any time of the day or night, often from people who want an animal or a bird or even a snake rescued or removed from their house. Some of them are genuine distress calls, particularly the ones about snakes, but mostly they're from people who should be able to deal with the situation themselves, and they just don't know how. In some cases you can explain what to do on the phone and they cope quite happily, in others they're too frightened or upset to try and I have to go. If there's any doubt I go anyway, but it amazes me that so many people have the attitude that our wildlife are strange, dangerous creatures and won't go near them. You'd think Australians would know their own native species better than that – we've got no lions or leopards here, after all.

'Other people sometimes ring us for advice about an animal or bird they're trying to raise, and you know that whatever you tell them will be useless because they think they know better. Hamish answered a call one day and I timed him on the phone for fifty four minutes, patiently telling a woman over and over again what to do with some animal. I could tell by his voice that she was one of the "Oh, yes but…" brigade and wondered how long he'd stand it. In the end he said, Madam, why did you ring me?'

'There was a silence and I knew he was getting an indignant answer, then he said, "I've been on this phone for almost an hour telling you what to do and you don't want to know. All you can say is 'But....' Goodbye." He put the phone down quite gently, and knowing Hamish I was amazed he'd been so polite.

'Very often the people who ring up and ask me for help aren't polite at all. They think Jirrahlinga's some kind of paid government service, set up just for their convenience. A man rang me about a seal that was tangled in a net at the bottom of a cliff. It was quite a long way from Jirrahlinga and when I got there he almost snarled, and said, "You've taken your time." He was really quite nasty, and it was a pretty scary rescue because the seal was on the rocks about a hundred feet down. I had to be lowered on a rope and swung sideways so that I could reach the seal, then hold onto it while they pulled me up again. We cut away the net and carried the seal to a proper beach to release it, and at least the man helped us. When it was all over he took me in his arms and hugged me.

'I wish we did get paid for rescues, it would be a great help financially. People ring up in the middle of the night or in the small hours, when I've just got to bed and I'm dead tired. I swing my legs out over the side of the bed when the phone goes, so that I won't fall asleep again. It's fine when the people who've called have a genuine problem I can help with, and they're really grateful. I've made a lot of friends that way and sometimes they give us a donation, but others behave as if I was a servant on call and I have to remind myself that I'm doing it for the animal. Those people don't really matter, you just forget about them.'

Rescue for the Layman

Tehree's rescue experiences are unlikely ever to come the way of the average citizen, but no Australian who ventures out beyond the city centre should go unprepared. Most people come across wildlife in need of rescue on country roads, cars being what they are and wildlife being so bad at avoiding them. In the worst case scenario the rescuer will also be the driver who has hit the animal and for most of us that's a trauma in itself, but anyone who drives on country roads, especially at night, should realise that it can happen. Cars have very little chance of avoiding an animal that suddenly appears in front of them from a dark roadside. Only the animal itself can be blamed for such accidents, but whatever species the victim may be an enlightened driver will stop the car, get out and do whatever's possible to help it.

Make a habit of keeping a few rescue essentials in your boot, a few old towels for a start. Even if you're spared the distress of hitting something car towels are an essential, and whether you find or create a road victim it will be in shock, needing to be kept both warm and immobilised while you find help. Carry a couple of old sacks as well, and if the animal is active and struggling put it into the sack so that it can't further damage itself, and always have a good torch in the glove box. As soon as possible ring the police who will direct you to the nearest wildlife carer, then take the victim to the carer who has the knowledge and the means to look after it. If there's a vet nearby he will help with its immediate problems, but the wildlife carer provides the expert nursing and rehabilitation. At Jirrahlinga Tehree runs a permanent casualty department, an animal hospital, a nursery and is prepared to deal with a multiplicity of injuries, diseases and exotic dietary needs.

There are some creatures that the ordinary person should leave well alone. Raptors and large seabirds such as gannets can inflict nasty wounds, both with their talons and their beaks. An injured snake is obviously a bad subject for amateur rescuers and seals, as Tehree says, only want to give their benefactor a serious bite. If you're convinced that any of these need help stand well back and call the police; they will pass the message on to the appropriate people. They may not be sympathetic in regard to the snake, but very few people do feel that way.

In the case of seals it's quite likely that the animal's not in trouble at all, either up on the beach to moult, to have a sunbath or, in the case of baby seals, to wait for Mum's return. The wildlife expert called on to travel a long distance, only to find a healthy, happy seal at the end of the trip, will not be pleased and the seal, unless it's sick or hurt, won't be pleased to see them either. If you can see nothing wrong with it, draw a line in the sand around it, write on a piece of paper 'THIS SEAL IS RESTING. PLEASE LEAVE IT ALONE' and peg it into the sand for the next would-be rescuer who comes along. The seal may appear to have tears running down its cheeks but that is the method by which seals wash the sand out of their eyes, and neither melancholy nor pain.

There are times when rescue attempts are useless because the victim is too badly damaged ever to be a whole, fully-functioning animal again. A koala with a severed arm or a kangaroo without a foot are both out of business in their separate ways of life, and a vet with a merciful needle is the best you can do for them. A neonatal marsupial, hairless, eyes still closed and ears pinned back, still attached to its mother's teat in the pouch will probably die by the time you've detached it from the teat and taken it to a carer. In the case of wildlife with severe injuries take it to the nearest vet who will put it down.

Tehree quotes the case of a woman, a mother with young children, who hit a Ringtail possum in her car near Lorne, an hour and a half's drive from Barwon Heads. There were three baby possums in the pouch so the woman driver, anxious to save them, phoned Jirrahlinga. Tehree asked her what size the babies were and, realising from her description that they were neonates, told the woman that their chances of survival were slim, and that she should go to a Wildlife First Aid worker or a Vet in nearby Lorne for help. Both the mother and her children were in such deep distress that Tehree's advice didn't get through to them. Instead they drove all the way to Jirrahlinga, wracked by misery, and by the time they'd got there one baby possum was dead and the other two subsequently died. Tehree estimates that the babies were only about two weeks old and their suffering was probably minimal, a matter of drifting into sleep. These neonates had a only a small chance of survival anyway, and the long drive had sealed their fate whereas quick help in Lorne, as Tehree had advised, might have made it possible to save one or more of them.

Another mistake common among rescuers of orphaned wildlife is the decision to take the baby home and raise it themselves. I have talked of this in earlier chapters, the fascination and growing affection for it, the inevitable errors in feeding and handling, the illness and death of the young animal and the rescuer's subsequent grief and guilt. Rather than risk that trauma, both for yourself and the animal, ring the police before you succumb to the creature's charms and ask them to direct you to the nearest wildlife carer. Keep the baby warm and comfortable until you hand it over and you will have saved everyone a great deal of suffering and sadness.

Then there's the importance of location, of always knowing the exact spot where you found the creature you rescued so that when it's released it can be returned to the same place. There are a number of reasons for this. Firstly, if the victim is a female there may be a baby close by, waiting for her return. A female echidna was brought to Tehree, injured but still lactating and Tehree, asked the woman who brought it exactly where she had found it. The woman, surprised, said, 'Somewhere along the Great Ocean Road. Why do you ask?'

'She's lactating. That means there's a baby waiting for her somewhere near where you picked her up. If we can get the mother back to the same spot quickly enough it may save the baby's life.' The woman rescuer hadn't realised the echidna was lactating, and anyway she'd been so intent on saving it that she hadn't really noticed where she'd found it.'

Anyone who rescues a wildlife victim, sick or injured, should pinpoint precisely the spot where it was found, because it's vital to return it to its home range where it will be familiar with the territory and its inhabitants. In the case of some birds which live in tightly bonded groups, kookaburras or magpies for instance, the arrival of a stranger is a threat and the newcomer may be badly hurt or even killed. Like the woman with the echidna people are often unaware of this, and so absorbed in the creature they've rescued that they take little notice of their exact location. Wounds can be cured, but release in the wrong place may be more disastrous in the end than the original injuries.

Tehree runs a professional animal rescue service which includes bushfire rescues during the summer and every other rescue imaginable throughout the year. Nothing surprises her any more, from being lowered down a cliff on a rope to rescue a baby seal to the removal of an enraged tiger snake from a suburban kitchen. These are not recommended exploits for ordinary citizens; you need knowledge of the species you're rescuing, its likely reactions and its physiology, and you need to be able to assess its injuries. Compassion is admirable, but you need expertise and common sense as well.

Release

The question of whether release is really successful applies to all hand-raised wildlife. Some species, and perhaps even some individuals, may cope more easily than others, but it depends mainly on the animal's pre-release preparation. Hand-raised kangaroos and wallabies, being herd animals, learn from their own kind in the wild. They must be kept with other young of their species in the period leading up to release, then released together with their friends. A mob of kangaroos will accept a pair of newcomers but may turn on a single individual whom they see as a threat to their established relationships. Once the youngsters have been accepted by a mob they complete their education by copying the behaviour of the wild kangaroos. As long as these animals are readied for release in the right way they have every chance of adjusting to the wild, but without that transition from the human to the animal world they will be rejected by the mob and unable to cope for themselves.

Wombats and echidnas are solitary by nature so that when they are released they must work out the encyclopaedic complexities of bush life on their own, but all hand-raised wildlife should know who and what they are before release. We may comfort ourselves that their instincts are strong enough to pull them through but we can't be entirely sure, and there is a very small margin for error in the bush. We raise our fostered wildlife with enormous care and affection but have we any idea of how they fare thereafter? Are we doing them a kindness or condemning them to misery? To put it bluntly, would we be kinder to have these orphaned baby animals put down, rather than raise them and then thrust them into a situation that may lead to misery, starvation or even death because they're unfitted for freedom?

Even animals that come into care as juveniles rather than babies can bond too closely with their carers. There was a young seal, one of the many that come to Jirrahlinga and as soon as possible return to the sea. Tehree says, 'The staff member who looked after her was having problems in her own life and she bonded with this seal, spent too much time with it and the seal became utterly dependent on her. When I realised what was happening it was too late; the seal was too humanised to be released. The staff member was very upset and said she'd learned her lesson. As it happened the seal died of an illness a little while later and it may have been the best thing for both of them in the end.'

In many ways the release of hand-raised wildlife is a more complex and demanding process than either their raising or rescue. Both the latter are wasted if their subject ultimately faces a miserable future because of, not in spite of, our loving human care. At a professional sanctuary such as Jirrahlinga preparation for release is an established routine, carried out according to the species involved and the individual creature's requirements. Registered Wildlife Shelters often work together in halfway housing mammals and birds with others of their own age and species to prepare them for release. People who raise singleton marsupials should contact a Shelter as soon as they are weaned, and arrange to have them halfway-housed with others of their own kind, fed natural food and given time to forget about their original carer.

'I'll give you an example of what happens when animals are over-humanised and then released before they're ready,' says Tehree. 'Take the case of a wombat called Waldo. He's with us at Jirrahlinga now and we have to decide what to do with him. Is he fit for release, should we get approval for him to stay in captivity or euthanase him?

'He was raised at a Shelter near Macedon, passed to another Shelter, then to a series of homes where he was allowed inside to sit on the sofa and watch TV, but suddenly, without any preparation for release, he was turned loose. He didn't think much of the bush, it was cold and dark and scary so he kept returning to civilisation, to houses with sofas and the telly. He liked humans and their comforts, and he thought it was where he belonged. Sometimes he was welcome, sometimes not, and finally he took to living under a caravan and following at the heels of the female occupant in an effort to be taken in and looked after. The woman, who wasn't a wombat fancier, was terrified of this strange monster and wanted him eradicated. Can you imagine how confused he must have been, poor Waldo? He must have wondered why the world had turned against him.

'A wildlife carer called Tracey heard about him and rang us at Jirrahlinga for help. He arrived with us in the back of a car, thoroughly enjoying the ride and greeted us like old friends, rolling on his back and wanting his tummy rubbed. He didn't like the look of wombat food but when we gave him a packet of chips, knowing what his lifestyle had been, he opened it at once and gobbled them. He's a lovely animal but he's convinced that he's at least part human because nobody's ever taken the trouble to teach him that he's a wombat. He can't handle wombat life. It's not his fault but unless we can rehabilitate him he has a limited future, and I'd hate to think it had to be euthanasia.'

The release of adult birds or animals that have been in care for a only a short time, because of illness or injury, is relatively uncomplicated once they have recovered and provided they go back to the location where they were found. The bird or animal will know his territory and be recognised there, problem bonding with humans will not have formed and the memory of past pain and trauma will fade.

'When we release possums that have come to us for any reason, injury, removal from houses or the hand-raised ones, we have to be very careful about two things. First, they have to be released in a suitable area and secondly they have to accept that territory as their own. We keep them in possum boxes for a few days before release with newspaper on the box floor so that they urinate and defecate on the paper. When we take them to the release location we leave them in the boxes and rub a likely-looking tree with the newspaper for each separate possum, then let each one go at the bottom of his own tree.

'You'll see them start to panic, then sniff their own scent and say to themselves, "That's strange, I've never been here before but that's my tree. I can smell me!" Then off they'll go up the tree, knowing it belongs to them.'

Tehree worries that no proper research has been done on what happens to hand-raised wildlife after release. She has a vet friend who has all but abandoned his practice to concentrate on wildlife because, he says sadly, so few owners of domestic pets should be allowed to own them. Together they hope to get funding for a research program to discover what happens to wildlife released after an infancy spent with humans. They hope to make a wombat the subject of their initial research because of its solitary nature and consequent vulnerability on release. These days we possess the technical means to follow a suitably tagged or implanted animal and to see if and how well it survives, but this costs money. Such observation could not be done by amateurs but would need professional and scientific expertise over a considerable length of time. Hopefully funding will be forthcoming because this is a question we need answered, both for the sake of the wildlife and for our own.

We really know very little about our wildlife except when they are in our care and human care is, at best, a totally artificial situation. Their physiology, their breeding patterns and their habitats are well and scientifically documented and magnificent wildlife films have been made of many of our native species. This is all fine but as the song says, nobody knows what goes on behind closed doors and once our hand-raised wildlife are released the doors close behind them.

Tehree is convinced that it is far better for people who acquire young wild creatures, raise them and love them as babies, to have them put down rather than release them, unprepared or into and unsuitable environment when they are grown. In the wild state an orphaned baby must die. A hand-raised animal's early life revolves round its carer and the loosening of their bond must be gradual, expertly managed and complete before it can have its freedom, and then it must be released in suitable surroundings. Far better to give it a lethal injection and a peaceful death while it's still happy and safe than utterly to break its heart.

Euthanasia

In the case of wildlife euthanasia is not simply a controversial last resort as it is with humans, but often the first and only act of mercy available to us. This means that when any damaged wild creature is found it is essential to take it to a vet or a carer who will assess its problems and pronounce the verdict of life or death. It's the only humane answer for birds that have lost their talons, marsupials that have lost a limb, echidnas with a crushed beak and a host of other sick or injured creatures that can never be restored to the wild. In their natural state they would die a prolonged and miserable death; we can help them best by taking them to a vet who will put them gently to sleep.

A great many people who believe themselves to be ardent animal lovers make the mistake of opposing the euthanasia of a badly injured animal, thereby prolonging its suffering. This is a mixture of ignorance and false sentimentality that amounts to cruelty, even though cruelty may be the last thing that person intended. Tehree must make the hard decision between life or death all too often in her work, and she knows that sentimentality has no place in the outcome.

A good example was the time when the Department of Conservation telephoned me at Kilmore. They told me that a man in a nearby country town had called them to say there was a seriously lame kangaroo on their Pony Club ground and that he and his neighbours didn't know what to do about it. 'We've been watching it there for a week,' he'd said, 'and it isn't getting any better. Could someone come over and get it?' They didn't tell me what size the kangaroo was but luckily I asked Russell Patrick, our Stud manager, to come with me. When I arrived at the pony Club ground there was a circle of men and women gazing at something in the grass. I walked past them and saw that it was a very large and emaciated female Eastern Grey kangaroo. One of her hind legs had been severed just below the hock and was held only by a trip of skin.

Russell and I got a blanket from the boot of our car, threw it over her and carried her back to take her to a vet for the only possible conclusion. She had been in great pain, under terrible stress and because she hadn't been able to move about to feed she was starving. As we loaded her into the car one of the bystanders tapped me on the shoulder and said anxiously, 'We've all been watching it for the last week and worrying about its leg. Can't you save it?'

The people who had been watching the 'roo were all good people, genuinely concerned but allowing sentimentality to swamp their common sense. You don't have to be a vet or a wildlife expert to understand that a kangaroo with one leg can never return to the wild, nor that if it can't move around it can't feed itself. Perhaps, in some muddled way, they imagined it could spend the rest of its life being hand-fed on a suitably constructed bed and that it would prefer that to death. This was a wild animal, already undergoing terrible suffering, and to add to that suffering the terror of being handled by humans would have been cruelty compounded. It's hard to believe that none of the roo's observers had a gun, common sense and compassion that avoided the pitfall of sentimentality.

Tehree is right in saying that education about our wildlife is the only way to preserve it, but people must want to learn. She does her best, with limited means and resources, to educate everyone she can reach about our wildlife and how to care for it, and she starts with small children. If a young child can touch and hold a wild thing, that moment stays in its memory and means something later on. Instead of just a picture in a book they will remember a paw or a bright, friendly eye, the texture of feather or fur. When that child becomes an adult it may think twice about going into the bush to shoot a friend, or leaving one to die on the roadside. It may even think twice about cutting down the trees wildlife live in, and systematically destroying their habitat until they can no longer survive.

Perhaps, some time in the future, schools may include wildlife care and habitat management in their curriculum as a serious subject, starting at primary or even at pre-school level. Visits by carers with their wildlife specimens, talks on raising, feeding and release and field trips to understand their environment would provide even the most city-bound child with a basic interest in wildlife and their preservation. The sad thing is that by the time our school system admits the necessity for such knowledge it may be too late.

Man makes excuses for himself and for his inability to live side by side with the flora and fauna of this planet without effecting its existence, all too seldom for the better. There are always more important things to think about, wars, money or politics and life in this world, other than our own, can wait. You may remember that song of the 'sixties, 'Where Have All the Flowers Gone?' which may well prove prophetic of the future. You may remember too the song's refrain, a question we should never stop asking ourselves, 'When will we ever learn, when will we ever learn?'

14 Reading Your Animal

THE ART OF READING your animal is not as mysterious as it sounds. Many people read their own dogs without even realising it, and most only have to apply it to a few domestic companions, cats, dogs or cage birds for instance. Horse trainers are either experts in the art or they are unsuccessful trainers. A good stockman reads his sheep and his cattle, both collectively and individually at a glance, or he loses his stock, while a lion tamer either reads his lions or he loses his life. The wildlife carer, in charge of a host of different species, must learn by experience enough of their separate languages to judge their health, their temperaments, their moods and their needs.

Tehree was the first qualified Dog Obedience Instructor in the Geelong area and her own dogs are totally responsive to her, a matter of mutual understanding and respect . She told me that when she was learning the art of dog obedience training she had an invaluable lesson from an expert named Michael Tucker who went out with her and her German Shepherd to coach her in tracking. She had the dog on a tracking harness in a paddock when it stopped abruptly at the base of a tree, looking into the air and whining. Annoyed, thinking it had lost concentration, she scolded it and tried to pull it away when a voice from above her in the tree said, 'You ought to be wearing the harness, not the dog. It was trying to tell you I was up here. *Learn to read your dog!.'*

'That was a good lesson,' Tehree says, 'and I've always remembered it. Actually, it's the same thing with all the wildlife. If you really study their behaviour when they think they're on their own you learn more about them than any other way. I spent about two weeks quite early on, just watching the koalas in their pen. There was a baby koala that threw tantrums like a child does, stamping and screaming and making life hell for its mother. She finally got fed up and gave it a sharp bite on its ear. It still didn't stop so she slapped it and that did the trick. It threw one of its tantrums with me when I was trying to do something with it one day. I held it out at arm's length but it still carried on so I thought, okay, we'll try what worked for Mum. I gave it a good bite on the ear and a little clip and it stopped at once, but I'd never have thought of doing that if I hadn't seen its mother do it.'

Animal behaviour is often misinterpreted by humans, and in most cases it's the animal that suffers. A good example was Jirrahlinga's Zeedonk, a cross between a Zebra stallion and a donkey mare, a combination guaranteed to generate behavioural problems. Zebras are notoriously difficult to domesticate or train and donkeys, as I know from experience, have minds of their own. Tehree's Zeedonk, who goes by the name of Zar, was born in the Melbourne Zoo in 1976, progressed to a donkey stud and then was sold to Koala Town, a Wildlife Park in Queensland. Tehree heard of Zar when Koala Town went bankrupt and the animals had to be dispersed, but Zar proved difficult to place. He was under sentence of death by a bullet when Tehree heard about him and offered to take him. He didn't come under the heading of Wildlife, but a Zeedonk sounded like an attractive Sanctuary exhibit.

Zar's trip from Queensland to Barwon Heads by horse float was apparently an epic journey, a convincing example of why Zeedonks are unlikely to become a chic and sought-after breed. In Zar's defence he'd been kept in a small enclosure at Koala Town, and that alone would have been a torment to the Zebra side of his nature. He was half herd animal after all, needing space and company and he was spoiling for a fight from the start after his solitary confinement. Horse float drivers pride themselves on their ability to deal with anything on four legs but on the whole they are used to valuable, well-educated thoroughbreds. They probably underestimated this pony-size, weirdly marked animal and treated him without respect. Zar, who had more of his father's temperament than his mother's, had the men on the proverbial ropes from the time when they first tried to catch him to put him on the float. Tehree was on the receiving end of a string of phone calls, increasingly blasphemous, before sheer weight of manpower overcame Zar and he was loaded. The float driver stated to Tehree that he would be delighted to supply the gun and the bullets to do what should have been done long ago, because the animal was mad.

'We have an overnight stop on the way down,' he said. 'I don't know what'll happen then.'

'Don't even try to take him off the float,' said Tehree sensibly. 'Put some food and water in with him and just leave him be.'

The next phone call, even more sulphurous, came from the overnight stop next morning. Some idiot had got him off the float by mistake and they were having hell's delight getting him on again, he was a bloody lunatic and he was making them late.

'Just keep trying,' said Tehree sweetly, and hung up.

The float finally arrived at Jirrahlinga in the dark and the apoplectic driver announced that he wouldn't go near the f….ing unnatural beast again, someone else would have to take him off. Hamish, a horseman all his life, was unimpressed by these horror stories. He advanced calmly into the float and moments later emerged with Zar, astonishingly quiet and obedient, walking beside him on a lead. The float driver departed, grinding his teeth.

Zar was put in a proper paddock where he had room to move but his behaviour was still distinctly anti-social. When someone approached his paddock he would charge the gate with his ears nailed back, grab it in his teeth and shake it until it almost came off its hinges. Friendly human advances were greeted with bared teeth and stamping feet. Tehree decided that two could play at the paddock gate game; she got to the gate before Zar did, seized the top bar and shook it as hard as she could while Zar backed off, his whole attitude expressing Zeedonk disbelief. After she'd repeated this performance a few times Zar kept away from the gate but he was still considered a risk, and the staff were told to take precautions whenever they went in to feed him.

Tehree was near his paddock one day when, to her horror, she saw a young and very new staff member walk into the paddock with his feed. 'I didn't dare call out to the girl in case she panicked,' she said. 'I just held my breath and watched.

'To my surprise there was no sign of aggression. The girl obviously hadn't heard about his reputation because she walked up to him, patted him and put his feed in his bin while Zar behaved as any pet pony might behave. He even rubbed his head against her. He followed her over to the gate and would have gone out with her but she just turned round to him, said "No" and he went off back like a lamb, back to his feed.

'It was a kind of revelation. We'd been treating him like a rogue because we'd been told he was a rogue and I suppose other people had been doing the same for years, just because they'd been told to be afraid of him. He'd felt that people were against him and responded in the only way he knew. This kid had just started work with us and she hadn't really heard about Zar. She shouldn't have been feeding him at all, but she went in to his paddock without any fear so he didn't feel defensive. It was the same thing the night he arrived, when he came off the float so quietly because Hamish treated him normally. Poor Zar, once we understood what we were doing wrong we could make it up to him.'

Zar is not an easy animal to love. To many people, it seems to have all the worst features of its parents, a donkey and a zebra. But at Jirrahlinga even a zedonk is 'read' and understood.

It was a classic example of 'Give a Dog a Bad Name,' and I wonder how often that happens with animals, simply because they're misunderstood. There's a lot of truth in the theory that dogs and horses are not born bad; instead that they're made bad or vicious by humans who, either unconsciously or purposely misunderstand them and maltreat them. Zar was a case of behaviour misinterpreted. He looked like a kind of horse so he was expected to act like a horse, whereas his personality and habits were predominantly Zebra.

Tehree said, ' He had a way of grabbing you by the shoulder with his teeth and shaking you and when we first got him it was pretty frightening. Then he'd lean against you and run his head down your leg as if he was going to bite your ankle so you'd react as if he'd done something wrong because you felt threatened. Then I watched a video about zebras in the wild. I watched it over and over again, and at last I understood what he was doing. In a zebra herd the shoulder grabbing and the leg rubbing are just their way of interacting socially, they do it to each other all the time. They bite each other's withers and shake each other and it's a kind of play, of zebra's being friendly, not savage, but whenever he did it we got cross and frightened. Donkeys are a bit like that too. Anyone who's tried to trim a donkey's feet would know that they'll cross their legs so you can't get at their foot and lean on you until they almost fall over. Zar's a combination of zebra and donkey and he's only doing what comes naturally.

'I told you about Splinter, the little kangaroo I rescued that had the mange and a broken tail? I remember her trying one day to tell me that something was wrong, and if I hadn't known her so well I mightn't have taken any notice. I saw when she came up to me that she was very worried, she was licking her forearms, which is always a sign of stress in a 'roo, and scratching at me, hopping away and looking back, so I followed her. There was another female kangaroo with a very small joey that had got out of the pouch and managed to get itself tangled up in a bush, it would have died if it had stayed there. The mother was an absolute idiot, she was nearby but doing nothing about it, just grooming herself. We put the baby back in her pouch and it was quite okay, but Splinter was the one who'd realised what was happening and come to tell me.

'It's just the same with domestic animals, dogs for instance, all owners should learn to read their dogs. I was standing in the front yard of the Sanctuary one day and to my surprise one of my German Shepherds bounded over the gate and came up to me, pulling at my jacket and barking. He knew that he wasn't allowed in the Sanctuary at all, so I knew something was wrong. He led me back to the house, by the quickest way incidentally, not the way he'd come, but straight to the swimming pool. We had about 35 penguins in there at the time and there was the younger German Shepherd, totally exhausted, 'rescuing' the penguins from the pool, taking them in his mouth and lifting them onto the pool's edge. Of course they'd jump straight back in again and the dog was so tired he couldn't even get out of the water himself. We had to lift him our and treat him for exhaustion. If the older dog hadn't told me to come quickly he'd have drowned but the penguins, I guess, thought it was terrific fun.'

Reading wildlife behaviour is far more difficult than reading that of domestic animals who live with us at close quarters, but for the wildlife carer it is essential. The signs by which Tehree assesses the health, temperament, moods and preferences of her charges are there for anyone to see, but only someone experienced in each particular species can interpret those signs. Many domestic pets bond with their owners so that each of them 'reads' the other without knowing that they're doing anything of the kind. Equally there are many owners who don't even try, and their pets must go to the grave wondering at the stupidity of people who have never understood them, no matter how hard the animal has tried to make them understand. You must learn, if you own a living creature, to admit that an animal can be right and you may be wrong, learn to concentrate on their reactions and their body language in different situations and to avoid the sin of believing that they can't communicate with you. Animals try to do that all the time, and it's up to you to meet them halfway.

15 Wildlife at Work

JIRRAHLINGA'S PERMANENT RESIDENTS are sometimes required to sing for their supper by appearing either in television productions or films. Whether or not the animals and birds involved regard this as an honour, or even mildly interesting, is hard to say. More probably they are deeply puzzled by this form of human eccentricity, but at least it means a contribution to the Jirrahlinga exchequer and Tehree sees that they come to no harm. In most cases, she says, the animals are treated with the greatest consideration by the Director and the film crew, if not she removes herself and her wildlife performers forthwith.

There's a widely held belief that wildlife can't be taught to act, that in order to catch them in the action demanded by the script you must spend hours of patient positioning and cajoling, with no guarantee of a positive result. A dog can be trained to perform any number of actions on command but this is simply not possible with a kangaroo or a wombat. Moreover, as Tehree knows well, the more any animal is asked to repeat even the simplest sequence the more bored and uncooperative it becomes, so she uses her knowledge of animal behaviour to short circuit the process. She quotes the case of a female kangaroo who was hired for a bush scene in a film. The location was a clearing in the bush surrounded by trees and she was greeted by a pleasant, understanding Director who clearly knew of the difficulties involved in camera work with wildlife.

'I expect this is going to take all day.' He said, 'But we'll just have to be patient.'

'What do you want her to do?' asked Tehree.

'I want her to come out from behind that tree, stand and look round for a few moments in a relaxed way, then hop to the middle of the clearing and graze for a bit, then stand up and look around. If she could look inside her pouch for a minute it would be terrific. I know it's going to take ages to get that sequence, if we ever do get it. It'll just be a matter of luck but let's try.'

'Show me where you want her to stop and graze.'

The Director took Tehree to a spot where she bent down and appeared to mark the ground. 'Right,' she said. 'I'll go back behind the tree with the 'roo and you tell me when you're ready to film.'

The camera crew, sighing at the prospect of a long haul, positioned themselves while Tehree and her kangaroo disappeared behind the tree and finally the Director called out 'Go!' The 'roo hopped composedly into the open and gazed round the empty clearing, sniffed the air and then hopped to the exact spot the Director had indicated, put her head down and grazed. After a few moments she stood up, looked down at her pouch, pulled it open and started to examine the interior. It was twenty-five minutes since Tehree and the kangaroo had arrived on location.

'I don't believe this!' said the Director. 'How the hell did you get her to do it?'

Tehree says, 'I never told him. He thought it was magic but it was chocolate, which she was mad about. I used to rub it round the inside edge of her pouch to teach her to clean it, because hand-raised 'roos don't know how to do that. In the wild they learn pouch cleaning from their mothers. When the Director showed me where he wanted her to stand and graze I planted a bit of chocolate under the mulch and while we were waiting behind the tree I rubbed a little bit in her pouch. She could smell chocolate and when I pushed her out into the clearing she put her head up and sniffed around, then hopped to the place where I'd planted it, and when she'd eaten that she cleaned up the chocolate in her pouch. It was a case of knowing animal behaviour and a bit of bribery.'.

White cockatoos are natural actors because they are addicted to showing off. Only a sick or unhappy bird of this species can resist making an exhibition of himself in company, and the bigger the audience the better. In this respect they are more promising subjects for a film career than marsupials, but their over-enthusiasm can make them unpredictable. Tehree took her personal pet cockatoo to a film assignment, confident that when called he would do her proud. He was a prolific talker with a large vocabulary, and he picked up new words fast. As it happened, filming that day was very slow and they sat on the sidelines waiting through endless retakes, the bird showing a lively interest in proceedings which, for everyone else, were

Building international relationships.

intensely boring. The Director was having trouble with a young actress who seemed incapable of getting her scene right and he was approaching boiling point.

'We'll do that again!' he yelled. 'For Christ's sake try to remember what I told you for once!' The girl was close to tears while all the rest, camera crew, extras and assorted workers were grinding their teeth and muttering under their breath.

Tehree and her cockatoo watched the unfortunate actress attempt her scene for the twentieth time, and it finally seemed that at last she was getting it right. Everyone held their breath, knowing that she was almost through and relief in sight when a voice, very like the Director's voice, yelled, 'CUT!' The cameras cut instantly, the girl turned white wondering what she'd done wrong this time, and the Director, purple with fury bellowed, 'Who the hell called Cut? I'll murder the bastard!'

Jirrahlinga supplies wildlife exhibits for conferences and functions, particularly for those where overseas VIPs are to be present, people whose schedule would otherwise give them no time to see our animals. Tehree loads her station wagon with a well-organised setting of bush foliage and suitable, seasoned wildlife specimens, usually a joey, a wombat and a koala. The bush setting is arranged in an appropriate corner of the function room and the animals, who enjoy attention and flattery as much as any of us, graciously receive the guests. Strictly speaking the work involved is all Tehree's and the animals simply have fun, but the appearance money they earn for Jirrahlinga comes in very handy.

Besides their work as actors or exhibits wildlife are becoming recognised as therapists for the old and the sick, indeed for anyone whose spirits are low and in need of comfort. Tehree has believed in animal therapy for a long time and applied it to hundreds of people, not only her Special People at the Sanctuary but in hospitals and Aged Care establishments as well. Domestic animals such as dogs, cats and cage birds have been acknowledged as therapists by the Medical profession for a long time, often as valued residents in Old Age Homes. It's hardly practical in such places to introduce resident kangaroos or wombats, but Tehree takes them in as visitors.

'It's amazing the effect they have on the old people,' she says. 'You know what those places are like when you go in, people sitting slumped in their chairs, looking miserable and bored. It's the same routine for them every day, just their meals and the TV and nothing left to look forward to, really. You come in with a joey or a baby wombat and they come to life, they start smiling and chattering and wanting to stroke it. It makes you feel good to see them and I wish I had time to do it more often.'

I know what she means. I took a little wombat to visit a young man I knew who was dying of Aids in the old Fairfield Hospital. The Aids ward should have been a miserable place, full as it was of doomed men hung about with tubes, ashen-faced, knowing what lay ahead of them. It was very quiet there too, until they saw the wombat. The man I'd come to see didn't have a chance; anyone capable of standing was out of bed, tubes and all and the incapable ones shouted at me to bring the wombat to them. We were there for some time and then the inevitable happened. The wombat, overcome by a surfeit of attention peed heavily down my slacks, turning them from white to sulphurous yellow, and wet into the bargain. It was the success of the day. The wombat and I retreated to the sound of applause and invitations to come again soon.

The wildlife at Jirrahlinga, both the temporary and permanent residents, are quite unconsciously working while they're there. Nobody, neither the visitors or more particularly the staff could quit Jirrahlinga without an increased appreciation of our wildlife. Tehree regards the Sanctuary as an educational tool as well as a refuge and a hospital, and she is fanatical in passing on her knowledge to the people who work with her.

She says, 'Our staff come to us from all walks of life. We take trainees, some for as long as a year, from TAFE, Universities and Wildlife management courses and even nurses and vets come to us to get experience. What they learn here they'll pass on to others, and it all helps. We get people from overseas as well. They're recommended to come here by various institutions because we can give them hands on training and we can pass them on to other places, like Healesville for instance, for further experience. We had a lovely

Italian family here from Italy last year, Nada Pretna and her sons, Luka and Daniel. They spent a month working with us and they're dying to come back.

'I suppose you could say that the wildlife work for all the people who come to Jirrahlinga, including the staff who believe they're working for the wildlife. All sorts of people apply for jobs here. The good ones, the staff who stay with us and really learn, are marvellous. A lot of them are people who've retired after working at something else all their lives, but always wanting to do something with animals and they become the backbone of the place. We get some wonderfully dedicated young people too who really love animals and will probably go on to make a future with them. The wildlife work for them, in all sorts of ways. Of course we get problem staff like every other employer, but you have to expect that and deal with it when it happens. Some people come here because they have a totally wrong idea of what our work's all about. They think that all they'll have to do is mess about with cute, furry animals, then they find out that the work's not only hard but dirty as well, and sometimes distressing, and those people can't wait to back out.

'The wildlife do wonders for what I call our Special People, the intellectually disabled, and we run a number of programs for them. They come to us in groups from places like Karingal and Barwon Valley Manor and they have a supervisor or a carer with them all the time they're here. Our staff are all trained to work with the carers and help them, and over time they've formed lasting friendships both with the carers and the people they care for. There seems to be some special relationship between the wildlife and the intellectually disabled, they trust each other instinctively.'

Jirrahlinga is a constant source of therapy for Tehree's Special People when they go there. Both grown-ups and children whose limitations have made normal social life with other humans difficult or impossible, find that the wildlife accept them without hesitation. Even if they do no more than sweep paths and deliver food to cages there's an ease of communication between themselves and the animals that they've never had with people. Rob Helmor, an English-born Instructor who brings a group from Karingal to Jirrahlinga every week, talked about the effect the visits had on them.

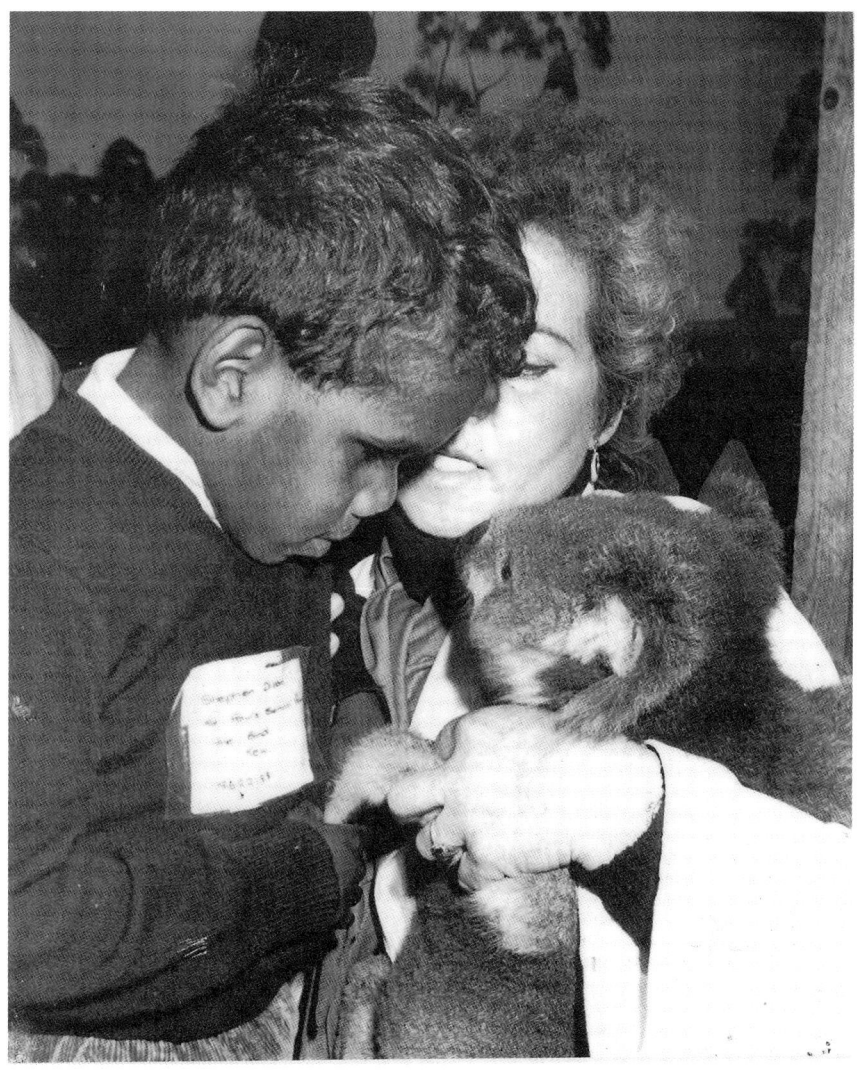

Tehree shows a blind boy how to 'see' a koala with his hands.

He said, 'There are different levels on which they can interact with the animals, according to the extent of their disability. At the higher level they'd love the animals to death if they could, and they enjoy any work they can do with them. The more severely disabled don't seem to really be aware of the wildlife or even interested if the bird or animal's asleep or motionless, but if it moves or makes a noise, then they're fascinated. They all love coming here though, if you say the word 'Jirrahlinga' at Karingal they're all jumping about, wanting to go there straight away.

'They do simple jobs here, raking paths and so forth and the love it. One of the most important things for them is approval, praise for something well done, so we give them things within their various capabilities and lots of applause. Tehree's wonderful with them. She can read these people as well as she can read wildlife and she knows just how to help them.'

Again on the therapeutic level, Tehree has established some of her young and convalescent wildlife in one most unusual environment, namely a high security prison where they're doing an excellent job as rehabilitation therapists. Barwon Prison was built about ten years ago not far outside Geelong, a somewhat bleak establishment on flat, featureless land, it's back turned to the world. Having seen the effect of wildlife on the aged, the handicapped and on troubled souls in general Tehree decided that prisoners came into the category of troubled souls.

Over a period of eight years and a succession of Prison Governors she submitted proposals for a scheme combining lectures by herself and suitable wildlife to be kept at the prison, cared for by the prisoners. One after the other the Prison Governors declined the idea, with varying degrees of politeness. It wouldn't work, they said. It would create trouble among the inmates, animals couldn't be kept in that environment because there was nowhere to put them, it would mean more work for the prison officers and, finally, the prisoners would abuse them or kill them. They pointed out that these were hard men, not pensioners or children. In the end Tehree gave up until one day, going through a file, she came on the Governor's phone number. 'One more try,' she decided.

Again there was a new man in the job and this time he listened. 'What kind of animals were you thinking of keeping here?' he asked. 'I like wildlife.'

'What do you like best?'

'Wombats,' he said. 'I love wombats.'

'Exactly what I had in mind,' said Tehree.

Shortly afterwards she was invited to go to the prison to talk about her program to the Governor and to choose suitable animal accommodation. When she first told me about the project she was excited but a little nervous because she had no idea what to expect, either from the prisoners or the prison staff. A high security prison is a sealed environment, of necessity inward looking and unwelcoming to those on the outside. Recently I went to Barwon Prison with her to see for myself. When we arrived we were signed in, given passes and waited for our escort to the Animal Nursery to arrive. Tehree is well known there now but she never moves beyond the reception point on her own.

'I was told to have a prison officer with me always, for my own sake,' she said. 'Then nobody can say I've dropped a packet of drugs somewhere or slipped something to a prisoner. Not everyone in here likes the wildlife program and they wouldn't hesitate to try and get rid of me by saying I'd done something like that.'

When she started the wildlife program it was with four carefully screened prisoners. She talked to the four men on the first day, with no idea at all of how the project would be received.

'I said to them that I wasn't coming to them as a do-gooder just to keep them occupied but because I wanted their help. I told them about Jirrahlinga and said that I had more young animals there than I could cope with because they need so much time and trouble, that I wanted a place where there was always someone on the spot to feed them and clean their cages and so on. They laughed at that, because they knew they weren't going anywhere. And I said they couldn't have the very young ones that had to be fed at night because they're locked up at five o'clock and they can't have animals in their cells. I said I'd teach them how to build cages and how to feed and look after the animals, that I'd bring in the food for them and I'd give them proper lectures about wildlife care. The main thing was that it wasn't me trying to help them, they were going to help me.' It was a shrewd approach and it worked.

The Animal Nursery has been running now for two years; it has grown in that time and there are plans for it to grow further. The original little brick room they gave Tehree has another, larger room alongside and a new concrete floor laid for more animal accommodation. Half the first room is taken up by temperature controlled snake tanks, occupied by some very small Children's Pythons and one full-grown Olive Python. The other half of the room is lined with possum cages, immaculate and well designed, both those and the snake tanks constructed under Tehree's instruction by the prisoners themselves. In a fenced, grass enclosure outside, pockmarked with little shell-holes dug by wombats, they have their eye on more space for enlarging the project, the present pair of young wombats being confined in a secure wooden pen, moveable so that they can get fresh patches of grass.

John, bearded, paunchy and always smiling is the boss of the Nursery, delighted to see Tehree and to have a visitor. He extracted Olive the python from her tank, all eleven feet of her, and she climbed energetically from one to another of us. She was fat and heavy and John said proudly, "She's put on a bit of weight, hasn't she, Tehree?'

"She'd hurt her mouth,' Tehree explained. "She was in pretty bad condition when she came here but she's done really well. I'll take her home soon, John, and bring you a Carpet Python.'

The baby Children's Pythons, all from the same hatch, were nevertheless in three stages of growth, one large and robust, one like a piece of spaghetti and one somewhere in the middle. The smallest, Shoestring, had died. 'Watch him!' said John as I went to pick up the middle-size baby. 'He's a snappy little feller.' Sure enough he was squaring up for a bite, all ten inches of him, and indeed the species has a reputation for being short-tempered.

We admired the possums, Brush and Ringtail, in their beds made from the halves of footballs and lined with cloth, as comfortable a nest as a possum could imagine. They had all come to Jirrahlinga as orphans or patients needing treatment and were growing or convalescing in the greatest luxury. John elaborated on their individual vices and virtues with the passion and insight of a psychiatrist. When we went outside to the wombats I asked if looking after the animals had helped him. He threw his head back, spread his arms wide and said, 'It's everything to me, everything! I've been inside for eighteen years and this is the first thing that's made me feel human.'

'It makes you think, doesn't it, animals humanising people?'

He looked at me in surprise and said, 'That's beautiful, beautiful. I hadn't thought of it like that.'

We stood talking in the sun outside the prison kitchen, John, the prisoner, a male and a female prison officer, Steve and Jan, Tehree and myself. Around us were modern buildings and fenced grass areas; high, secure fencing, blank-faced, anonymous buildings and a feeling that the buildings had their backs turned on the world to exclude it, intent only on what was inside. A few green-uniformed prisoners moved about in ones and twos but on the whole the place felt empty, not so much of people as of normality, of life-as-we-know-it. This of course is the purpose of a modern prison, to create not the hell-hole prison of the past but a habitable, disciplined vacuum in which the wrongdoer can choose or refuse to be reformed. I asked how many of the prisoners wanted to join the program and both John and Steve, the prison officer, looked embarrassed. Steve said, 'Quite a lot would like to but we have to be careful,' and John said, 'They wouldn't be right for it, not the young smartarses. We had one guy come in and leave the door of a possum cage open. We made him hunt for it till he found it in the bottom of the frig and got it out. He had bruises from his chin down to his feet for that, and he was told that next time he did something careless he wouldn't even be breathing, we were that upset when it went missing.'

Steve said, 'I didn't believe in this program in the beginning, like a lot of the others here. I didn't think it'd last but now I'm a convert,' and Jan, who has been Tehree's prison mentor and guardian since the beginning declared, 'it's great. It can only get bigger.'

One of the things John said was that Tehree's talk to them the first day had grabbed them. 'Nobody ever asks you to do something for them in here, not like that, not like you could actually do something worthwhile. We couldn't believe it was true.' There was the fascination of building animal houses, of information about wildlife and learning something new. Then the animals themselves and Tehree bringing their food, frozen mice for the snakes and so forth, but most importantly giving them the responsibility for these living things. If John is an example of what the program can mean to the men inside it's more than worthwhile. I've no idea what he's already done eighteen years for or how long he has to go, but he's clearly happy in his work and avid to learn more.

Tehree told me that when she was going through the prison to the Nursery one day with Jan there was an 'incident', alarm bells, whistles and scurrying warders. Jan said calmly, 'Don't worry, we just have to stay exactly where we are and we'll be okay.'

The next week one of the prisoners sidled up to Tehree and said, 'There was an incident when you was here last week, wasn't there?' She said yes, and he went on, 'Don't worry about nothing here, you'll be quite safe, no-one will hurt you. The word's gone out on you, you see.'

I asked John what would happen if anyone in the prison deliberately harmed one of the animals. He looked shocked, as though the question should never have been asked. 'I hate to think what would happen to him,' said John. 'He'd have a very short future.'

The beauty of all this is that the wild creature involved has no idea that it's actually working, much less that in many instances it's helping the human race. If they are unhappy in their work, as in the case of repetitive film sequences, they will make their point in an unmistakable manner; either by just switching off or possibly by biting someone, while the therapeutic work gives them obvious pleasure. Praise and appreciation works wonders, for Special People, ordinary people, wildlife and all other creatures, just the same.

In other countries bears are made to dance, tigers and lions to jump through hoops and monkeys to ride bicycles, all too often taught by very unpleasant methods and always for some human's financial gain. Thankfully Australians have never attempted to make wombats or kangaroos do any of these things, nor do I believe they'd be successful if they tried. Our wildlife has been allowed to keep its distance from such indignities, and the work it unwittingly does for us has far more value than mere circus tricks

16 So You'd Like to Run a Sanctuary?

THE LAYMAN may not appreciate what it means to run a sanctuary such as Jirrahlinga, housing not only healthy wildlife but also providing for a multitude of sick and injured creatures, orphans and convalescents. A zoo has the same logistical problems of the feeding and accommodation of a host of species, but not of the constant arrival of patients needing treatment and eventual rehabilitation. These notes are based on methods used at Jirrahlinga, some of them Tehree's own, many of them common to a number of other sanctuaries, and they may give some idea of the complex ities involved. Since most Wildlife Sanctuaries and Shelters deal primarily with sick, injured and convalescent creatures we'll start with instructions on the feeding of the convalescents.

Feeding convalescents

Koala Glug (for malnourished and convalescing koalas)

Basic mix:

4 scoops Divetelac to 80 ml pre-boiled water

1 flat tablespoon vanilla Sustagen or a 1 inch strip of Nutrigel

1 flat tablespoon of high protein cereal (e.g. Heinz)

Add a strip of Probotic (promotes healthy gut flora).

- It is possible to substitute electrolyte mix for water if the animal is dehydrated.
- A little stewed apple may be added to the mix and then blended well, so that it will go through a syringe.
- Tehree's pumpkin soup and her addition of a Berocca tablet for dehydrated animals is mentioned in Tehree's advice on raising koalas (see chapter 6).

To administer:

- Use a 20 or 50 ml syringe, placed in the mouth and directed towards the throat.

- The animals usually like the taste and sallow it readily so feed until it seems satisfied and repeat feeding as required. Tie a bib round the koala because the Glug sticks like glue and flush the mouth out after feeding with a small amount of water or electrolyte mix from a syringe.

Possum Glug (for weaned possums)

1 scoop Biolac to 80 ml pre-boiled water

1 flat teaspoon vanilla Sustagen or half-inch strip of Nutrigel

1 flat teaspoon high protein cereal.

Mix well and feed by syringe or on spoon.

Macropod Glug: (for kangaroos and wallabies).

- This is much the same as Koala Glug but with some additional ingredients suitable for macropods. It can be fed to malnourished animals or those with fractured bones, but never to an animal that you have to chase in order to administer it. Chasing will cause stress and further damage.
- As well as the ingredients for Koala Glug, Macropod Glug can include stewed apple, cooked carrot, rice cereal, wheatmeal biscuits and rolled oats It can be fed with a syringe or a spoon (hopefully the animal will like the taste) but never so fast as to make the animal choke.
- Flush the mouth out after feeding to prevent bacteria. When it is well enough to move about a little feed it with grated apple and carrot and cooked rice. Always have water available for it.
- The Glug can be fed for 3–4 weeks but it is not a natural diet so watch for diarrhoea, constipation, skin problems and stress related symptoms. If any of these occur consult a vet.

Wombats

A mixture of horse muesli with some high protein baby cereal and Divetelac sprinkled on top. If the wombat refuses to eat you can put it back onto the bottle or syringe Divetelac into its mouth, but be careful not to get bitten. If the wombat is just weaned it will take the bottle readily and even adults will take the milk formula if they can't eat for reason of injury, but add Lectade or electrolyte to their drinking water. Macropod and Koala Glug can be fed to adult wombats.

Echidnas

In short term care they can be fed a mixture of 2 scoops Divetelac, 100 ml water and 2 eggs, beaten. Heat the mixture in a double saucepan until it is custard consistency and feed it in a shallow bowl or in the palm of your hand.

Birds (for birds too sick to eat on their own).

Seed eaters:
- Offer an egg and biscuit mix or a commercial granivore mix.
- You may have to crop feed them (with a special syringe which delivers the food directly into their crop) until they can eat on their own. Offer them natural food as soon as they show signs of doing so and supplement with crop feeding until they are eating normal quantities.

Meat and fish eaters:
- Can be force-fed with their natural food, meat or fish. If they regurgitate their food you may have to give them small, frequent feeds throughout the day.
- Raptors need extra calcium and either fur or feathers combined with their meat, the natural roughage they would get with their prey in the wild.

Honey eaters:
- If they don't want to take solid food feed them a normal commercial honey mix.

Insect eaters:
- Feed a slurry of commercial insectivore mix.

Fruit eaters
- Ripe soft fruits which can be mashed to a consistency useable in a syringe if necessary.

With all convalescent birds small, frequent feeds are better than occasional large feeds.

Supplements

These are particularly necessary for sick or injured birds and can be obtained from vets.

- Most birds like Nutrigel and both this and vanilla flavoured Sustagen can be mixed with food preparations.
- Probotic, which promotes natural gut flora, especially if the bird or animal is on anti-biotics, is another product to have on hand.
- Others to be kept in stock are charcoal tablets, electrolytes, worming remedies, external parasite treatments, constipation and diarrhoea medicines.

Equipment:

This is a very basic list but if you are to treat or care for wildlife you must have:

- heat pads
- hot water bottles
- weighing scales
- suitable cages
- warm, natural fibre bedding
- feeding utensils such as crop needles and syringes
- animal teats and bottles for wombats and macropods. These teats can be bought at some chemists, or from vets.

You will also need a basic wildlife First Aid kit and for this you should consult a vet or an established wildlife carer. Surgical rubber gloves and face masks should always be included in your equipment.

Hygiene:

This is important both for the wildlife and the carer.

After feeding an animal clean round its mouth with a mix of a half ml of tea-tree oil and half a cup of water to prevent bacteria forming. You can use the same mix to wipe its bottom, especially when the animal is unable to move around and to urinate and defecate normally.

You must always keep its feet, its bottom and its bedding clean.

Cleaning Products:

Antibacterial solutions:

- Miltons – powder and liquid – for soaking both feeding and medical utensils and for washing bedding.
- Hibiclens (Scrub): Medical strength disinfectant. Wash your hands with this after and between treating animals and use it to clean minor wounds.
- Chlorex and Avisafe: for disinfecting cages and equipment.
- Salt water (1 heaped teaspoon salt to 100 ml water): Boil feeding and medical equipment in this for five minutes, then rinse.

If you run a Shelter or a Sanctuary you must be prepared to cater for everything. Some Shelters do specialise in one particular species of animal or bird and have immense expertise in dealing with that species, but all Shelter Permit holders take whatever turns up; they learn to expect the unexpected and to deal with it. When you are as large and well-known for wildlife care as Jirrahlinga your occupancy book covers most of the State's birds, mammals and reptiles, including aquatic birds and mammals. It should be some comfort to Tehree that crocodiles are not native to Victoria, because if they were she'd undoubtedly have to rescue them, take them in and care for them.

The recipes for convalescents given above cover only a few of the many species catered for at Jirrahlinga, and then only in basic outline. Not included is advice on species such as snakes and seals which require specialised, expert handling, but Tehree must provide for them as well. Add to the convalescents the sick and injured new arrivals, the hospital equipment and medication, the food and accommodation for the permanent residents and you will begin to understand that running a sanctuary is definitely not for the fainthearted.

Tehree's Routine (and yours, if you run a Sanctuary)

A normal day for Tehree begins at 5 am. This doesn't vary simply because she's been called out for a rescue during the night, there are babies to be fed at two to three or four hour intervals and the staff won't arrive until 8 am. Before that she must have a shower and a cup of coffee, settle the babies and do what she can in the office.

At 8 am there's a meeting when the staff are told their duties for the day. Tehree spends the morning looking round the sanctuary, checking on the wildlife, the maintenance, the staff and a dozen other details, phoning a vet for advice about the animals in the hospital and doing more admin work in the office. There are bills to be paid, food and equipment to be ordered, her educational work to be planned and the inevitable records to be kept for the DNRE. After lunch-on-the-run the work continues. Sanctuary staff have their problems as any staff do and these have to be settled, often requiring tact and lengthy counselling, the education of the trainees attended to and the arrival of new patients coped with.

The staff finish work at 6 pm, leaving Tehree with the orphaned wildlife, herself and her husband to be fed, the normal domestic duties of a household to be coped with and hopefully a few hours sleep before it all starts again. Her sleep depends on the absence of phone calls for help or a rescue, and on how many baby animals require two-hourly feeding. That's the routine for an average day and very few of them are average, furthermore she works a seven day week with no days off. You still want to run a Sanctuary?

The Rescue Service

This is a project which the average person shouldn't and wouldn't even consider. However, since Tehree run's a professional Animal Rescue Service her list of standard equipment may be of interest.

Safety Equipment:

- Barrier cream (hands)
- First aid kit (gasic)
- Gloves (plastic, rubber & leather)
- Snake bandage

Clothing (personal)

- Hard hat
- Uniform/overalls
- Safety jacket
- Name badge
- Identification (driver's license)

- Leather belt & pocket knife
- Keys on chain clip
- Leather boots
- Change of clothes
- Wet suit/waders (sea rescues)
- Weather proof hat & coat

General equipment

- Safety glasses
- Belt torch & hand torch
- Cyalume Light stick
- Compass
- Water proof matches
- Knapsack
- Whistle
- Fire blanket
- Dog clips
- Honey (Manuka – medical properties)
- Water bottle

Animal needs

- Heat blanket/hot water bottle
- Bottles & teats
- Towels & bandages
- Animal First Aid kit
- Transport crates or bags
- Hartmann's fluid & syringes
- Tranquilliser gun/capture guns
- Gun, ammunition, cartridges – guns to be kept locked away separately in vehicle.
- Licenses for guns

Vehicle Kit

- Torch

- Compressor
- Water/coolant
- Spare fan belt
- Tow rope
- Jump leads (heavy duty)
- Witches hats – safety bollards – warning
- Flashing light triangle
- Tarps
- 2 animal transport trailers

Tool Kit

- Pliers
- Bolt cutters
- Chain saw/bow saw
- Plastic body bags
- Snake hoop bag
- Snake stick or snake hook
- Rescue bags (all sizes, ties attached)
- Assorted nets
- Extension catching poles
- Climbing gear (harness & ropes)
- Assorted stretchers

Throw that little lot together before you get in the car to answer a call, and don't forget anything!

Hospital Equipment:

Jirrahlinga is far from typical of the average Shelter in terms of hospital equipment. Because of its size, its rescue operation and the diversity of its wildlife it must be prepared to deal with almost anything, usually at short notice. In Tehree's words, 'We have a bird hospital, a koala hospital, a general hospital and nursery and in them incubators, humidicribs, heat boxes and specially made koala hot water bottles. We have surgical gear and sterilisers, medications, bandages and all the things necessary for surgical dressings and treatment of illnesses. Our hospitals have tiled floors and stainless steel tables, and the vet is on call seven days a week. We need an X-ray machine very badly, and maybe some day somebody will donate one. We need a dart gun too, for anaesthetising injured animals we can't catch, but we can't afford either that or the X-ray machine yet.

'No small Shelter would need equipment as elaborate as ours but you should have cages or an aviary for birds, pouches for orphaned marsupials, hot water bottles or heat pads and you should always have a supply of Divetelac or Wombaroo on hand for young animals that arrive suddenly. You'll need bottles and teats, towels and some soft sheepskins, bandages and disinfectants and of course a Wildlife First Aid Kit. Ask your vet about the First Aid Kit and he'll help you to put one together. When the young animals are being weaned they'll need proper enclosures, both to protect them and to keep them from destroying your house or your garden. Baby's play-pen will come in handy, but you'll need heavier, wire mesh ones as well.

'There's always an ongoing need for maintenance in a place that houses animals and birds, cages and enclosures get damaged, new ones have to be built and you never get to the end of it. We're very lucky here at Jirrahlinga because we have wonderful voluntary maintenance men who look after it for us. We'd be out of business if it weren't for our volunteers, they do all kinds of things for us as well as maintenance. They are really wonderful people. So are our staff. They don't have a 'nine-to-five' attitude to their work; they really love the creatures they look after and if there's any kind of a crisis they'll work until they drop.

'There's a good network between the Wildlife Shelter people too. We try to communicate, to exchange information and experience and generally to help each other out. If one Shelter has a windfall of something, it could be a donation of hessian or something useful for maintenance, they'll contact other Shelters to see if they need the same thing, and share it. And remember, Shelter people are always ready to help other people who help wildlife by raising them and caring for them.

'When I'm lecturing I often quote the experts who say, "The saving of one animal of a common species does nothing for the environment, or for the survival of that species", but I wonder how true that really is. There are many Australian native species which were common enough two hundred years ago and have disappeared completely now. Think of the wildlife that must have been wiped out in the New South Wales bushfires last year, let alone the constant erosion of the species that seem plentiful these days, by our destruction of their habitat. We'll wake up sometime in the future and find them gone.

'Australia must learn to manage its wildlife for the long term, to protect it and to make sure that it has the habitat in which it can survive. In the short term we, the Wildlife carers, do what we can. We save whatever we can save and return them to the bush to live and breed, we reduce their suffering when they're sick or hurt, we live with them and learn from them and we're happy for them when they can go back. It's hard work and there's heartbreak as well as joy in it, but I truly believe that the wildlife deserve our help, that it's all worthwhile.'

R.I.P.

Under the Environment Protection and Biodiversity Act of 1999 the following number of wild species are classified as Extinct, Endangered or Vulnerable. This is the latest statistic available. It is up to us to ensure that by the time we get a new assessment of our wildlife the endangered species have not become Extinct, the Vulnerable have not joined the Endangered and been replaced by a list of new members of the Vanishing Wildlife Club.

	Birds	*Mammals*	*Reptiles*
Extinct		24	27
Endangered	34	33	12
Vulnerable	60	31	38